move Up

Pre-intermediate
Student's Book A
Simon Greenall

Editorial Consultants

Bridget Green Mukogawa Fort Wright Institute
James Hunter Gonzaga University English Language Center
Institute for Extended Learning, Community
Colleges of Spokane

MACMILLAN
HEINEMANN
English Language Teaching

Map of the Book

Lesson	Grammar and functions	Vocabulary	Skills and sounds
Progress Check Lessons 6–10	Review	Word chains Compound nouns Categorizing vocabulary	**Sounds:** syllable stress in words; /ð/ and /θ/; /ɒ/ and /əʊ/; friendly intonation **Writing:** predicting a story from questions **Speaking:** talking about past events; families
11 *How Ambitious Are You?* Talking about ambitions	Verb patterns (2): *to* + infinitive; *going to* for intentions, *would like to* for ambitions	Ambitions Verbs and nouns which go together	**Reading:** reading and answering a questionnaire **Writing:** writing a paragraph describing your ambitions using *because* and *so*
12 *English in the Future* The role of the English language in the future of your country	*Will* for predictions	Jobs School subjects	**Listening:** listening for main ideas **Sounds:** syllable stress in words; /e/ and /eɪ/ **Speaking:** talking about the future of English
13 *Foreign Travels* Planning a trip to South America	*Going to* for plans and *will* for decisions Expressions of future time	Equipment for travelers	**Listening:** listening for specific information **Speaking:** planning a trip
14 *All That Jazz* Finding your way around town	Prepositions of place Asking for and giving directions	Town features Adjectives to describe places	**Reading:** reacting to a passage **Listening:** listening for specific information **Sounds:** /æ/, /ə/, /ɑː/, and /eɪ/ **Speaking:** giving directions around town
15 *An Apple a Day* Typical meals in different countries	Expressions of quantity: countable and uncountable nouns, *some* and *any*, *much* and *many*	Food and drink Meals	**Listening:** listening for specific information **Speaking:** talking about typical meals and food in different countries

Fluency 3 *The Cost of Living*   **Numbers and prices**

Lesson	Grammar and functions	Vocabulary	Skills and sounds
Progress Check Lessons 11 – 15	Review	Word maps Nouns from verbs and nouns from other nouns Noun suffixes for jobs	**Sounds:** weak syllables /ə/; /tʃ/, and /ʃ/; contrastive stress; polite intonation in questions **Speaking:** planning a lunch party for friends
16 *What's On?* Typical entertainment in different countries	Prepositions of time and place Making invitations and suggestions	Types and places of entertainment and related words	**Listening:** listening for specific information **Speaking:** talking about typical entertainment **Writing:** writing and replying to invitations
17 *Famous Faces* Describing people	Describing appearance and character: *look like, be like*	Words to describe height, age, looks, build, and character	**Speaking:** describing people **Writing:** writing a letter describing your appearance
18 *Average Age* Personal qualities at different ages	Making comparisons (1): comparative and superlative adjectives	Adjectives of character	**Reading:** reacting to a passage and comparing information in a passage with your own experience **Speaking:** talking about exceptional people **Writing:** writing sentences describing exceptional people
19 *Dressing Up* Typical clothes in different countries	Making comparisons (2): *more than, less than, as … as*	Clothes Colors Personal categories for organizing new vocabulary	**Reading:** reading for specific information **Sounds:** weak syllables /ə/; weak forms /ðən/, /əz/, and /frəm/; stress for disagreement **Listening:** listening for main ideas **Speaking:** talking about clothing
20 *Memorable Journeys* A car journey across the United States	Talking about journey time, distance, speed, and prices	Numbers Words to describe a long-distance journey by car	**Listening:** listening for specific information **Sounds:** syllable stress in numbers **Speaking:** talking about a memorable journey

Fluency 4 *Special Occasions*   **Saying dates; saying the right thing**

Lesson	Grammar and functions	Vocabulary	Skills and sounds
Progress Check Lessons 16 – 20	Review	International words Adjective suffixes Male and female words	**Sounds:** /ʊ/ and /uː/; /dʒ/; polite and friendly intonation **Speaking:** pair dictation **Writing:** pair dictation to recreate a story

1 | *Welcome!*

Present simple (1) for customs and habits: questions; adverbs of frequency

SPEAKING AND LISTENING

1. Work in pairs. Where do you hear these words and phrases?

in a bar   in a store   in a hotel   at home   in class

Hello.   Goodbye.   Pleased to meet you.   Thank you.
How do you do?   Can I help you?   How much is this?
Fine, thanks.   I'd like a Coca-Cola.   How are you?
I don't understand.   Could you repeat that?   Sorry!
Come in.   This is my friend Rosario.

2.  What's happening? Listen and find out where the people are.

3. Put the words in the right order and make questions.

1. first your what's name
2. do live you where
3. are married you
4. do do you what
5. and you brothers sisters do any have
6. from where come do you

What's your first name?

 Now listen and check.

4. Go around the class greeting people and asking suitable questions.

READING

1. *Make Yourself at Home* is about hospitality in Saudi Arabia, the United States, and Japan. Read it and match these headings with the paragraphs. There are three extra headings.

a. type of clothes   b. length of stay   c. refreshments
d. special customs   e. gifts   f. topics of conversation
g. time of arrival

2. Which paragraphs are true for your country?

Make Yourself at Home

1. "In my country, men usually go to restaurants on their own. They always take their shoes off before they go in. Then they usually sit on the floor around a small, low table. In the evening they often sing songs."

2. "We always offer our guests something to drink when they arrive, tea, coffee, or perhaps water or soft drinks. We think it is polite to accept a drink even if you're not thirsty. If you visit someone, you always stay for a few drinks. When you have had enough to drink, you tap your cup or put your hand over it. If you say no, your host will insist that you have more to drink."

3. "It's difficult to know when to leave, but an evening meal often lasts about three or four hours. When the host serves coffee, this is sometimes a sign that the evening is nearly over, but you can have as much coffee as you want."

4. "If the invitation says eight o'clock, we never arrive exactly at eight. We arrive about ten or fifteen minutes later. But you never arrive before eight."

GRAMMAR

> ### Present simple (1) for customs and habits
> **You use the present simple to talk about customs and habits.**
> *In my country men **go** to restaurants on their own. They **take** their shoes off.*
>
> **Negatives**
> *He **doesn't** live here. You **don't** take wine. We **don't** arrive early.*
>
> **Questions**
> **There are two types of questions:**
> **– with questions words:** *who, what,* etc.
> ***What's** your first name?*   ***How are** you?*
> **– without a question word**
> ***Are** you married?*   ***Do** you **have** any brothers and sisters?*
> **You can answer this type of question with** *yes* or *no*.
>
> ### Adverbs of frequency
> **You can use adverbs of frequency to say how often things happen.**
> *They **always** take their shoes off.*
> *We **usually** offer our guests something to drink.*
> *It **often** lasts about three hours.*
> *We **never** arrive early.*

1. Complete these sentences with verbs from the passage.

  1. In my country we ___ at a table for our meals.
  2. We usually ___ ten or fifteen minutes after the time on the invitation.
  3. People ___ coffee at the end of the dinner party and then they ___.
  4. Men often wear a suit when they ___ to a restaurant.

2. Write a question for each heading in *Reading* activity 1.

  a. type of clothes: What do you wear to a dinner party?

3. Look at *Make Yourself at Home* again. Underline the verbs which are with an adverb of frequency.

WRITING AND VOCABULARY

1. Choose seven or eight verbs from the box and write sentences about hospitality in your country. Include a suitable adverb of frequency.

| accept arrive ask answer come from drink earn give go know |
| live offer put say send sit sing stay take take off talk about |
| think visit wear want |

  We usually offer a cup of coffee when guests arrive.

2. Look back at the questions you wrote in *Grammar* activity 2, and write answers for your country.

2 *A Day in the Life of the U.S.A.*

Present simple (2) for routines: third person singular; expressions of time

READING AND VOCABULARY

1. Read *A Day in the Life of the U.S.A.* and decide who you can see in the photos.

2. Work in pairs. Say what you usually do at the times mentioned in the passage.

At 6:30 A.M. I'm still asleep.

I also have lunch at 12:45 P.M.

3. Match the verbs with suitable nouns in the box.

> start television come dinner
> leave have stop lunch watch
> breakfast home get school
> finish work

start school, start work, ...

4. Say what time you do these things.

> get up get dressed go to sleep
> take a shower/bath wash

I get up at seven thirty.

A Day in the Life of the U.S.A.

6:30 A.M., Poughkeepsie, New York. Norman Davies, 37, gets up and takes a shower. After breakfast, he washes the dishes and then drives to the station. He works in New York City, and the commute takes an hour, so he hurries to catch his train.

10:30 A.M., Long Beach, California. Tony de Valera takes a coffee break between meetings. He works for the Disney corporation as a designer.

12:45 P.M., Evanston, Illinois. Thirty-four-year-old Amelia Noriega, head of public relations for a major car manufacturer, stops work and has lunch with a friend. "There aren't many women at my job level," she says.

4:30 P.M., Tampa, Florida. George Markopoulos, 65, comes home after his daily swim. Then he joins his wife at the community center, where she teaches aerobics.

5:00 P.M., Seattle, Washington. Jo-Ann Rosenthal leaves work. It's Friday night so she walks to a local bar and meets her friends.

7:45 P.M., Lubbock, Texas. Cliff Renton III, 51, gets ready to go out to the local Ranch Handlers' Ball.

11:00 P.M., Athens, Georgia. Shirlee Lewis finishes dinner, does the dishes, and watches the news on TV. Her five children are asleep, so she tries to be very quiet.

GRAMMAR

> Present simple (2) for routines: third person singular
> **You use the present simple to talk about routines.**
> *He **gets up** at 6:30.*   *She **works** in Seattle.*
> **You form the third person singular (*he/she/it*) of most verbs in the present simple by adding -*s*.**
> *He get**s** up at 6:30.*   *She work**s** in Seattle.*
> **You add -*es* to *do*, *go*, and verbs which end in -*ch*, -*ss*, -*sh* and -*x*.**
> *He wash**es**.*   *She go**es** to school.*
> **Verbs which end in a consonant + -*y* change to -*ies*.**
> *carr**ies**   fl**ies***
> **The third person singular of *be* is *is*. You often use the contracted form '*s*.**
> *It**'s** Friday night.*
> **The third person singular of *have* is *has*.**
> *She **has** lunch with a friend.*
>
> Expressions of time
> *in* the morning
> *in* the afternoon
> *in* the evening
> *at* night
> *before* lunch
> *after* dinner
> *at* about seven o'clock

1. Write down the third person singular of these verbs. (You can find them in the passage.)

come   drive   finish   get   hurry   join   leave   meet   say   stop   take   teach   try   walk   wash   watch   work

2. Put the verbs in three columns.

-s	-es	-ies
gets	*finishes*	*hurries*

Now add these verbs to the correct column.

do   dress   fly   go   live   make   carry

LISTENING

1. 🔲 Listen and decide which people in *A Day in the Life of the U.S.A.* are speaking.

2. 🔲 Listen again and find out what they do at these times:

Speaker 1: 8:00 A.M.   1:00 P.M.   5:00 P.M.   11:30 P.M.

Speaker 2: 8:15 A.M.   12:30 P.M.   5:30 P.M.   7:00 P.M.

3. Work in pairs and check your answers.

At 8:00 A.M. ___ leaves home and goes to work.

SOUNDS

1. There are three different ways of pronouncing the final -s in the third person singular present simple.

🔲 Listen to these verbs. Is the final sound /s/, /z/, or /ɪz/? Put them in three columns.

takes   goes   finishes   sits   sings   arrives   refuses   offers   has   asks   talks   serves   washes   watches   does

2. Now say the words out loud.
🔲 Listen and check.

SPEAKING

Work in pairs and find out about your morning routines. What time does your partner do these things?

– wake up   – get up   – get dressed   – have breakfast
– go to work

Noriko, what time do you wake up?
I wake up at seven o'clock.

What time do you get up?
At a quarter after seven.

What does the word "home" mean to you? How do you say the word in your language? We asked some people about their homes.

What's the main room in your home?

"The kitchen, because it's warm and we have breakfast, lunch, and dinner there seven days a week."
Jackie, Sydney, Australia

What are typical features of homes in your country?

"In the United States, houses almost always have a garage. In fact, most new houses in the suburbs have a two-car garage, and sometimes even a three-car garage! We love cars!"
Pat, Los Angeles, U.S.A.

Do you have a television? If so, where?

"In the bedroom. We like to watch it in bed."
Ya Fang, Taipei, Taiwan

If you live in a town, do you stay there on weekends?

"Well, we live in the center of New York, but only because I'm an architect and I work there. I really wouldn't call it home—that's what I call our house in the country where we go every weekend."
Elizabeth, Connecticut, U.S.A.

Do you lock your door when you go out?

"In cities we do. Although when I was a child in the Elburz mountains, we left the door open. And if we found a visitor or a traveler wandering in the street, we always invited them in." **Sharock, Teheran, Iran**

How often do people move home in your country?

"In the United States many people move about every ten years."
Cheryl, Boston, U.S.A.

So *home* means a lot of different things to different people. What does it mean to you?

VOCABULARY

1. Look at the words in the box and find *two types of housing* and *five rooms*.

apartment bath bathroom
bed bedroom carpet
chair closet dining room
dishwasher door drapes
house kitchen lamp
living room refrigerator
shower sink sofa stove
table toilet video
washing machine window
yard

2. Work in pairs. In which rooms do you find the furniture and equipment in the box above? Which word is left?

3. Work in pairs. Ask and say what rooms there are in your homes.

Is there a living room?
Yes, there is.
Is there a dining room?
No, there isn't.

Now ask and say what furniture and household equipment there is in your home and where it is. Add words to the lists if you can.

There's a table and some chairs in the kitchen.

Is there a video? No, there isn't.

READING

Read the passage and think about answers to the questions for your country.

GRAMMAR

> **Articles**
> **You use the indefinite article *a/an*:**
> – **to talk about something for the first time:** *There's **a** kitchen and **a** dining room.*
> – **with jobs:** *I'm **a** teacher. She's **an** engineer.*
> – **with certain expressions of quantity:** ***a** little food   **a** few beds   **a** couple of friends*
>
> **You use the definite article *the*:**
> – **to talk about something again:** *In **the** kitchen there's a table, and on **the** table there's a cat.*
> – **with certain places and place names:** ***the** Alps   **the** West   **the** United States*
> – **when there is only one:** ***the** president   **the** government   **the** weather*
>
> **You don't use an article:**
> – **with plural and uncountable nouns when you talk about things in general:**
> *It has carpets and curtains. There's lots of food.*
> – **with certain expressions:** *at home, at work, in bed, by car*
> – **with meals, languages, most countries, and most towns:**
> *Let's have lunch. Speak English. We live in Brazil. I lived in Quito.*
>
> **Plurals**
> **You form the plurals of most nouns with *-s*:** *chair – chair**s**   cupboard – cupboard**s***
> **You add *-ies* to nouns with two or more syllables which end in *-y*:**
> *balcony - balcon**ies***
> **You add *-es* to nouns which end in *-ch, -ss, -sh,* and *-x*:** *church - church**es***
> **There are some irregular plurals:** *man – men   woman – women   child – children*

1. Look at the articles and phrases underlined in the passage. Which of the rules about articles in the grammar box do they illustrate?

2. Complete the sentences with *a/an, the,* or put - if there's no article.

1. Last year we moved to ___ Los Angeles.
2. ___ kitchen is ___ door on your left.
3. ___ weather is very hot in August.
4. There isn't ___ table in ___ kitchen.
5. Would you like ___ drink?
6. I'm sorry, he's still at ___ work.

3. Write the plural of these nouns.

parent house city family dish party bush country table fax feature

SPEAKING

1. Work in pairs and look at the photo. What room do you think it is? Does it look like a room in a house in your country?

2. Work in pairs and talk about your answers to the questions in *Home At Last*.

3. What does the word "home" mean to you? Write five words or phrases which you associate with the idea. Find out what other students in your class wrote.

4 *First Impressions*

Verb patterns (1): *-ing* form verbs; talking about likes and dislikes

First Impressions

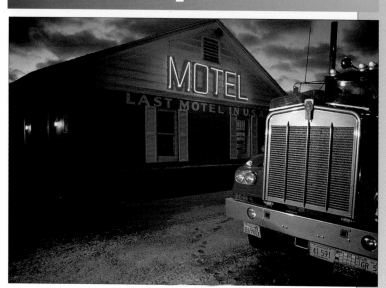

The British and the Americans speak the same language. But life in the two nations can be very different. We asked some Americans what they like or don't like about Britain...

"The police. They're very friendly, and they don't carry guns." Claude, Trenton

"The weather is awful. You don't seem to get any summer here. It's winter all year around." Toni, San Francisco

"The tourists! It's so crowded. I think you should do something about them. And I can't stand the litter everywhere. It's very dirty." José, Washington

"Feeling safe when you walk the streets. Oh, and the polite drivers who stop at a crosswalk if they see someone waiting there." Moon, Los Angeles

"Driving on the left. It's very confusing. I keep looking the wrong way." Paula, San Diego

So then we asked some British people what they like or don't like about the United States...

"Arriving at the airport. Immigration is so slow, it takes hours to get through!" Geoff, London

"The people, they're so generous. If they invite you home, you're sure of a big welcome." Amin, Bath

"Going shopping. I love it. It's so cheap everywhere—food, clothes, hotels, petrol." Paul, Oxford

"I hate the insects. They're so big. In Texas the mosquitoes are enormous. But I suppose in Texas they would be!" Maria, Glasgow

"Driving on the right. It's very confusing. I keep looking the wrong way." Sandra, St Albans

READING AND VOCABULARY

1. Read *First Impressions*, which is about people's impressions of Britain and the United States. Put a check (✓) by the positive impressions and a cross (✗) by the negative impressions. What is the most surprising impression?

2. Underline the adjectives in the box.

awful big cheap confusing crowded dirty drivers driving food friendly
generous gun immigration insect police polite shopping slow tourist
weather winter

Now write them in two columns, *positive* and *negative*, according to their meaning in the passage.

Can you remember which nouns they went with in the passage?

3. Look at the words in the box. Put a check (✓) by anything you particularly like and a cross (✗) by anything you dislike.

Think of two or three things that people like and dislike about your country.

GRAMMAR AND FUNCTIONS

Verb patterns (1): *-ing* form verbs
You can put an *-ing* form verb after certain verbs.
*I **love** walk**ing** She **likes** swimm**ing**.*   *They **hate** ly**ing** on the beach.*

Talking about likes and dislikes
Questions
***Do** you **like** the weather?*   ***Does** he **like** the police?*
***Do** you **like** walking in the park?* ***Does** she **like** the weather?*

Short answers
*Yes, **I do**. Yes, he **does**.*   **No, I** *don't.* **No, she** *doesn't.*

Negatives
*I **don't** like the weather.*   *He **doesn't** like arriving at the airport.*
*We **don't** like insects.*   *She **doesn't** like driving on the right.*

Expressing likes
I love it.
I like it a lot.

Expressing dislikes
I hate it.   I can't stand it.
I don't like it at all.

Expressing neutrality
It's all right.   I don't mind.

Expressing the same likes and dislikes
I like rock music.   So do I.   Me, too!
I don't like jazz.   Neither do I.   Me, either!

Expressing different likes and dislikes
I like rock music.   I don't.
I don't like jazz.   I do.

1. Do you like or dislike these things? Respond to the statements.

1. I like going to parties.
2. I don't like cooking.
3. They like walking.
4. I don't like insects.
5. He doesn't like tennis.
6. She likes shopping

1. I don't.

2. Look back at the passage and say what the people like or dislike and why.

Claude likes the British police because they're friendly and don't carry guns.

SOUNDS

Listen to the way these people use a strong intonation to express strong likes or dislikes.

1. I hate the insects
2. I can't stand the litter.
3. He loves shopping.
4. I like the people very much.
5. She doesn't like driving on the left.
6. He hates the tourists.

Now say the sentences out loud.

SPEAKING

1. Write down four or five things you like about your town or country, or the town where you are now.

2. Find people in the class who like the same things. Now talk about things you don't like.

3. Tell the rest of the class about your likes and dislikes. Make two class lists: the *Top Five Likes* and the *Top Five Dislikes* about your town or country, or the town where you are now.

Present simple and present continuous

SPEAKING

1. Work in pairs. Take a closer look at your partner! How much do you know about each other? Guess the answers to these questions.

Does he or she...

- play a musical instrument?
- paint or draw?
- ride the bus often?
- smoke?
- work hard?
- speak a foreign language?
- listen to music?
- earn a lot of money?

I think she plays the piano.

2. Now ask and answer the questions about each other. Did you guess correctly in 1?

Do you play a musical instrument?   No, I don't.

3. Look at the *yes* answers. Is your partner doing these things at the moment?

Is he working hard?   Yes, he is.

Is she smoking?   No, she isn't.

4. Look at the photos. Choose one person in each photo and take a closer look. Imagine what his or her life is like and guess the answers to the questions in 1.

I think he/she plays a musical instrument.

GRAMMAR

> **Present simple**
> **You use the present simple to talk about:**
> – a habit   *He smokes twenty cigarettes a day.*
> – a personal characteristic   *She plays the piano.*
> – a general truth   *You change money in a bank.*
> **There is an idea that the action or state is permanent.**
>
> **Present continuous**
> **You use the present continuous to say what is happening now or around now.**
> *It's raining.   He's drawing a picture.   I'm learning English.*
> **There is an idea that the action or state is temporary.**
>
> **You form the present continuous with *is/are* + present participle (verb + *-ing*).**
> *I'm looking at the photos. She's waiting for a bus.*
>
> | **Questions** | **Short answers** | **Negatives** |
> |---|---|---|
> | *Is he drawing?* | *Yes, he **is**. No, he **isn't**.* | *He **isn't** drawing.* |
> | ***Are** you going home?* | *Yes, I **am**. No, I'm **not**.* | *I'm **not** going home.* |

1. Work in pairs and point at the people in the photos. Ask and say what they're doing at the moment and why.

What's the man in front doing?   He's playing the accordion.

Why is he playing the accordion? Maybe he doesn't have any money.

2. Look at these verbs in the present participle and write their infinitives.

drawing getting having making playing shopping putting staying

draw get …

What happens to infinitives ending in *-e, -t, -p,* and *-y* when you form their present participle?

3. Complete these sentences with *and* or *but*.

1. I often go shopping at the supermarket ___ I'm going there now.
2. They usually eat at home ___ today they're having dinner in a restaurant.
3. She walks to work ___ this week she's taking the bus.
4. He smokes ten cigarettes a day ___ he's smoking a cigar right now.

SOUNDS

[cassette] Listen and check (✓) the phrase you hear. Is the underlined sound /n/ or /ŋ/?

1. carry <u>in</u>/carry<u>ing</u> an umbrella
2. sitt<u>ing</u>/sit <u>in</u> there
3. sing <u>in</u>/sing<u>ing</u> tune
4. arrive <u>in</u>/arriv<u>ing</u> time
5. take <u>in</u>/tak<u>ing</u> money
6. stand <u>in</u>/stand<u>ing</u> there

Now say the phrases out loud.

LISTENING AND VOCABULARY

1. Say where you do these things:

buy plane tickets   get some medicine have dinner   change money   buy food
Choose from these places.

bank   drugstore   post office   restaurant grocery store   travel agency

2. [cassette] Listen to four conversations and decide where the people are. Choose from the places in 1. Now work in pairs. Say where the people are and what they're doing.

3. Look at the words in the box. Are they nouns, verbs, or both?

> bank bus buy change close cross draw food get grocery store hold line look at medicine money paint pharmacist play post office put railroad station rain road shelter shop sit stand stay street suitcase take think ticket town umbrella wait for   walk

4. Group any words which go together.

bank, money…

Fluency **1** *Good Morning!*

Greeting people; asking for information in the classroom; giving instructions in the classroom

LISTENING AND READING

1. Read this dialogue and decide whether you would hear it in a classroom in your country. When does it take place?

KELLY Hello, Joe. How are you? Have you eaten?

JOE Hi, Kelly. Fine, thanks. Yes, I've eaten. Hey, you look great today! That's a beautiful dress.

KELLY Thanks. How was your weekend?

JOE OK.

TEACHER Good morning, everyone. My name is Steve Smith. You can call me Steve. How are you all today?

JOE Hi, Steve! We're all fine.

KELLY Good morning, Mr. Smith. Very well, thank you.

TEACHER Please sit down, everyone. Isn't it a beautiful day?

DAVE Oh, I'm sorry I'm late. Excuse me!

TEACHER No problem, we've just started. Now, take out your textbooks and turn to page 15. No talking, please.

JOE Can I ask a question? Can you tell me what *Buenos dias* means?

TEACHER I'll answer your questions later. It means *Good day* or *Hello* in Spanish. OK, I'd like you to work in pairs.

DAVE Oh, not again. Is it OK if I work with you, Kelly?

KELLY Yes, of course.

2. Work in pairs and check your answers.

3. 🔲 Listen to the dialogue in 1 and cross out anything you don't hear.

4. Work in groups of four and act out the dialogue you heard.

FUNCTIONS

> ### Greeting people
> *Good morning.*   *Good afternoon.*   *Good evening.*   *Hello.*   *Hi!*
> *How are you?/How's it going?*   *Fine, thanks, how are you?*
>
> ### Ways of addressing people in spoken English
> *sir*   *ma'am*   *Mr. Smith*   *Steve*   *Ms. White*   *Mrs. Jones*   *Mary*
>
> ### The alphabet
> Aa Bb Cc Dd Ee Ff Gg Hh Ii Jj Kk Ll Mm Nn Oo Pp Qq Rr Ss Tt Uu Vv Ww Xx Yy Zz
>
> ### Asking for information in the classroom
> *How do you spell ___?*   *Can you tell me what ___ means?*
> *What does ___ mean?*   *How do you say* Buenos dias *in English?*
> *Could you repeat that, please?* *Could you speak more slowly?*
> *How do you pronounce this word?* *Is it OK if I work with you?*
> *Can I ask a question?*

1. Work in pairs. Which ways of greeting people do you use in your English class?

2. Which ways of addressing people do you use in other classes in your country?

3. How many letters does the English alphabet have? How many letters does your alphabet have?

4. 🔲 Listen and repeat the alphabet.

5. Put the letters of the alphabet in the right column.

/eɪ/	/iː/	/e/	/aɪ/	/əʊ/	/juː/	/ɑː/
A	B	F	I	O	Q	R

🔲 Now listen and check.

6. Match the two parts of the exchange.

1. Is it OK if I work with you?
2. Can you spell that?
3. What does *sayonara* mean?
4. Could you repeat that, please?
5. How do you say *Hello, how are you?* in Spanish?

a. It's Japanese for *goodbye.*
b. Yes, I said "Work in pairs, please."
c. S-M-I-T-H.
d. You say *¿Hola, qué tal?*
e. Sure.

READING AND LISTENING

1. Read and answer the questionnaire.

2. 🔊 Listen to an American answering the questionnaire and take notes about her answers.

3. Work in pairs. Compare your notes in activity 2.
🔊 Now listen again and check.

SPEAKING AND WRITING

1. Work in pairs and talk about your answers to the questionnaire. Are your answers very different from the American's answers?

2. Write a description of what happens at the beginning, during, and at the end of a class in another subject in your country. Compare it with an American language class.

In my country we stand up when our teacher comes in the room, but in the United States...

1. Do you greet people when you come into class? If so, what do you say?

2. Do you stand up when your teacher comes into class?

3. What do you call your teacher?

4. Do you say you're sorry if you're late?

5. Who should talk most in a language class, the teacher or the students?

6. Do you only speak when you're spoken to?

7. Do you expect to work with other students?

8. Do think it's all right to cheat sometimes?

9. Do you ever ask questions during the class, or do you wait until the end?

10. Which of the following do you expect in your language lessons?

quizzes   exams   dictionaries   reference books
exercises   songs   role-plays   textbooks   translation
pair work   field trips   written work   speaking practice
games   pronunciation practice   listening practice

11. Which do you expect in lessons on other subjects?

12. How do you know when a class is over?

13. Do you wait for the teacher to leave before you leave?

VOCABULARY

1. Look at this crossword.

Work in pairs. Choose words in the vocabulary boxes from Lessons 1 – 5 and put them in a crossword. How many words can you find?

2. Some words can be more than one part of speech. For example:

*cook: a **cook** (noun) is someone who **cooks** (verb) food.*
*orange: an **orange** (noun) is an **orange** (adjective) fruit.*

Use your dictionary to find out what parts of speech these words can be.

talk   head   drink   fly   start
rent   slice   heat

Write sentences showing their different parts of speech.

He talks all the time.
There's a talk on insects tonight.

3. Not every new word is useful to you. Look at the vocabulary boxes in Lessons 1 – 5 again and choose ten words which are useful to you.

Start a *Wordbank* in your Practice Book for useful words and phrases. Write the ten words in your *Wordbank*.

GRAMMAR

1. You meet Tanya, from Russia, at a party in New York. Here is some information about her. What are the questions?

1. I live in Moscow.
2. Yes, I am and we have three children.
3. I am a scientist.
4. I start work at eight in the morning.
5. I finish at six in the evening.
6. In the evenings we have dinner.
7. On weekends we go to the country.
8. We usually go to a beach on the Black Sea.

1. Where do you live?

2. Put an adverb of frequency in each sentence so that it is true for you or your country.

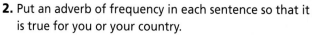

always   (not) usually   (not) often   sometimes   never

1. We take off our shoes before we go into a house.
2. We offer guests something to eat.
3. We talk about politics and our families.
4. We have dinner at seven o'clock.
5. We give the hosts some wine or flowers.
6. We sit on the floor.
7. We wear nice clothes.
8. We arrive ten or fifteen minutes late.

3. Answer the questions with one of these expressions:

Yes, I do.   No, I don't.   I love it.   I hate it.
Not very much.   It's OK.   Not at all.

1. Do you like living in a town?
2. Do you like shopping?
3. Do you like walking?
4. Do you like hot weather?
5. Do you like warm beer?
6. Do you like fast food?

4. Write the *-ing* form of these verbs.

close   visit   fly   wear   make   sing   get   throw   cross   go   stay   cut

5. Choose the correct verb form.

1. Tanya *comes/is coming* from Russia.
2. She *visits/is visiting* New York.
3. She *takes/is taking* a vacation.
4. She *speaks/is speaking* English quite well.
5. She *stays/is staying* with friends in New York.
6. She *enjoys/is enjoying* her visit.
7. She *goes/is going* shopping most days.
8. She *says/is saying* she wants to come back soon.

6. Complete these sentences with *a/an*, *the*, or put - if there's no article.

1. There's ___ radio in ___ living room.
2. Would you like ___ cup of ___ coffee?
3. They have ___ large house in ___ country.
4. We have ___ son and ___ two daughters.
5. ___ children are outside in ___ yard.
6. What's ___ main room in your apartment?
7. She spoke ___ very good Spanish on ___ phone.
8. I flew to ___ Montana and spent ___ two weeks in ___ Rockies.

SOUNDS

1. Say these words out loud.

does   finishes   gets   goes   leaves   looks   refuses
sings   smokes   wants

Do they end in /s/, /z/, or /ɪz/? Put them in three columns.

▶️ Now listen and check.

2. ▶️ Listen and say these words out loud.

<u>ea</u>t   <u>i</u>t   f<u>i</u>fteen   f<u>i</u>fty   l<u>i</u>ve   l<u>ea</u>ve   s<u>i</u>t   s<u>ea</u>t

Is the underlined sound /ɪ/ or /iː/? Put the words in two columns.

3. ▶️ Listen to these questions. Put a check (✓) if you think the speaker sounds interested.

1. What's your name?
2. How old are you?
3. Where do you live?
4. Do you live with your parents?
5. Are you married?
6. Is that your brother?
7. Is that your husband?
8. Do you have a sister?

Now say the sentences out loud. Try to sound interested.

SPEAKING AND WRITING

1. Look at some rules for punctuation in English.

1. You use a capital letter:
   – at the beginning of a sentence: *I like cake.*
   – for names: *Sue Jim Elaine*
   – for the first person singular pronoun: *I*
   – for nationalities: *She's American.   the Koreans*
2. You put a period at the end of a sentence:
   I don't speak Japanese.
3. You put a question mark at the end of a question:
   Do you speak Spanish?
4. You put quotation marks and a comma around someone's actual words:
   "I'm Mexican," he said.
5. You put an apostrophe for contractions:
   I'm American.   He doesn't live here.

Now punctuate these sentences.

1. we dont usually visit people without an invitation
2. when we meet people for the first time we say how do you do
3. when do you use first names in your country
4. your friend is called jim smith do you call him jim or mr smith
5. its usual to use first names with people when you get to know them

2. Work in groups of three or four. Talk about customs and traditions of hospitality in your country. Talk about the following:

Invitations:	Do you ever visit people without an invitation?
Greetings:	How do you greet people when you meet them for the first time?
Names:	When do you use first names, family names, or titles?
Punctuality:	When do you arrive for an appointment?
Clothing:	What do you wear for a lunch or a dinner engagement?
Food and drink:	What food or drink do you expect?
Conversation:	What do you talk about? What don't you talk about?
Compliments:	Do you make compliments about the food, the host's house, or personal objects?
Leaving:	When do you leave a dinner party?

3. Write some advice for visitors to your country about customs and traditions of hospitality and entertainment. Write about the points in 2 and say what people do or don't do.

6 Expensive Toys

Past simple (1): regular and irregular verbs

VOCABULARY AND READING

1. Look at the large photo and describe what you can see. Can you guess what it is and where it is?

2. Look at the words in the box. Which are nouns and which are verbs? Can any be both?

> bridge build check cost
> cross fit lead name
> principle ship smile spend
> trip

3. The passage is by Charles Kuralt, an American travel writer. Read it and find out if your guess in 1 was correct.

4. Are these statements about the passage true or false?

1. Robert P. McCulloch isn't very rich.
2. He built Lake Havasu City in Colorado.
3. The London Bridge cost $7.5 million.
4. They put the bridge up over the Colorado river.
5. People didn't believe that the London Bridge was in the Arizona desert.

Robert P. McCulloch is a millionaire. In the 1960s, he built his own dream town in the Arizona desert, beside a lake fed by the Colorado river. But after he finished it and named the town Lake Havasu City, and filled it with streets and houses and golf courses and all, he still did not feel satisfied. The city needed something else. Robert P. McCulloch thought the London Bridge would be nice.

So he wrote a check for two and a half million dollars, and he bought the London Bridge.

He shipped it over from the River Thames in London, England, every stone of it, and put it up in the Arizona desert. However, the bridge didn't have a river to cross, so Robert P. McCulloch made the Colorado river flow under the London Bridge. The whole project cost him about $7.5 million.

More than a million people make a special trip every year to see if it's true that the London Bridge is now in Arizona. It's true. People drive across the London Bridge and look out at the lake and the desert and smile.

These are English stones, but the principle that brought them here is American—the principle that if you have five or six million dollars to spend, well, what you spend it on is entirely up to you.

Adapted from A Life on the Road, by Charles Kuralt

GRAMMAR

> **Past simple (1)**
> **You use the past simple to talk about a past action or event that is finished.**
> *The city **needed** something else.*
> *He **wrote** a check for two and a half million dollars.*
> **You form the past simple tense of most regular verbs by adding -ed.**
> *start -start**ed**   He started by building his own dream town.*
> *finish - finish**ed**   He finished it.*
>
> **Many verbs have an irregular past simple form.**
> *write - wrote   buy - bought   be - was/were*
>
> **Negatives**
> *He still **did not** feel satisfied.*
> *The bridge **didn't** have a river to cross.*

1. Look at the passage again. Find the past simple of these verbs

buy cost finish name need put think write

Which verbs are regular? Which ones are irregular?

2. Look at the past simple form of these regular verbs and write their infinitive form.

carried closed continued danced decided liked lived stopped traveled tried

What's the rule for forming the past simple of regular verbs ending -e, -y, -p, -l?

3. Look at the past simple form of these irregular verbs and write their infinitive form.

became came chose cost cut did hit had heard knew made met put ran read said shut took told understood went wrote

4. Which verbs in 3 have the same form in the present and the past simple? Which verb has the same form but sounds different?

SOUNDS

1. 🔲 Listen to the pronunciation of the past-tense endings of these verbs.

/t/	/d/	/ɪd/
liked	lived	decided
washed	stayed	visited

Put these verbs in the correct column.

continued finished enjoyed started walked danced called wanted expected

2. 🔲 Listen and check. What's the rule? Now say the verbs out loud.

SPEAKING

1. Work in groups of three or four. Do you think buying the London Bridge and moving it to Arizona was a waste of money? Why do you think Robert P. McCulloch did it?

Maybe he...   Perhaps he...

2. Think about a very expensive thing you or someone you know bought. If you can't think of anything, make something up! Then tell your group about it. Give as much detail as possible: say why, where, and when you bought it, and how much you paid. The others will listen and then say if they believe you.

My mother bought a solid gold sink for our bathroom...

The World's First Traveler's Check

Past simple (2): questions and short answers

When you go abroad on vacation, how do you pay for things? These days, you can usually use a major credit card, but millions of people prefer to take traveler's checks because they know that banks and stores accept them wherever they go. Two people were responsible for the traveler's check: J. C. Fargo, the president of the American Express Company from 1881 to 1914, and one of his employees, M. F. Berry.

In 1890, J. C. Fargo decided to take a trip to Europe. He took a letter of credit from a leading American bank with him, which told foreign banks how much money he had in his bank account at home, and was the usual way for a traveler to finance his trip abroad. However, Fargo found that he had to wait a long time to get his money, and that many banks refused to give him money at all! This made him angry, and when he returned to the United States, he went to the office of M. F. Berry.

"Berry," he said, "I had a lot of trouble with my letter of credit. The moment I left the big cities, it was completely useless. If the president of American Express has that sort of trouble, just think what ordinary travelers have to put up with! Do something about it!"

For months, Berry thought about the problem, and in 1891 he found the solution. His invention, which he called the "Traveler's Cheque" (using the British spelling), was basically the same as today's version. When you bought an American Express Traveler's Cheque, you signed your name on the top line, and when you cashed it, you identified yourself by signing the bottom line. It was as simple as that.

The American Express Traveler's Cheque was an instant success with both American travelers and foreign banks, and it was soon popular worldwide. An example of this is the story of an American tourist in the Sahara Desert in the 1920s who wanted to buy a beautiful camel blanket from an Arab trader. The price was twenty dollars. The tourist pulled out the cash and offered it to the trader, but the Arab looked at the money and shook his head. The tourist then pulled out an American Express Traveler's Cheque, and the Arab, smiling and nodding, immediately gave him the blanket.

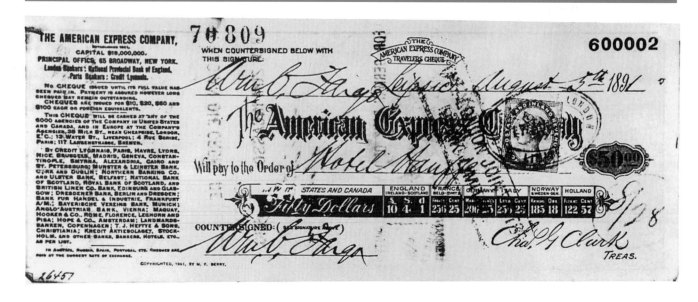

READING

1. Work in pairs. What are traveler's checks? How do you use them? What do they look like? Now read *The World's First Traveler's Check* and find out how the first traveler's check was invented.

2. Read these statements about the passage. Are they true or false?

1. M. F. Berry was the president of the American Express Company.
2. J. C. Fargo went to Europe in 1890.
3. J. C. Fargo had no trouble with his letter of credit.
4. M. F. Berry invented the traveler's check in 1891.
5. You signed the bottom line of the traveler's check when you bought it.
6. The traveler's check did not become popular for many years.
7. The American tourist wanted to buy a camel.
8. The trader wanted $20.
9. The trader didn't want to take a traveler's check.

GRAMMAR

Past simple (2)
Questions | **Short answers**

Was it easy to use the letter of credit? — *Yes, it was. No, it wasn't.*

Did he go to Europe? — *Yes, he did. No, he didn't.*

You can use *who*, *what*, or *which* to ask about the subject of the sentence. You don't use *did*.

Who invented the first traveler's check? — M. F. Berry.

You can use *who*, *what*, or *which* and other question words to ask about the object of the sentence. You use *did*.

What did he **call** his invention? — The Traveler's Cheque.

Compare:

Subject *Who **invented the** traveler's check?* — M. F. Berry.

Object *What **did** M. F. Berry invent?* — The traveler's check.

---

1. Work in pairs and check your answers to *Reading* activity 2.

1. *Was M. F. Berry the president of the American Express Company?*
   No, he wasn't.

2. Here are some answers about the passage. Write suitable questions.

1. J. C. Fargo.
2. In 1890.
3. A letter of credit.
4. Because many banks refused to give him money.
5. In 1891.
6. By signing on the bottom line.
7. In the Sahara Desert.
8. A beautiful camel blanket.

1. *Who was president of the American Express Company from 1881 to 1914?*

VOCABULARY AND SPEAKING

1. In the box below are some of the verbs from this lesson. What is the past simple of each verb?

decide find get give identify
look make nod pay pull out
refuse return shake sign
smile take tell think wait
want

Try to remember which words go with these verbs.

Decided to take a trip, found he had to wait...

2. Work in pairs. Tell your partner about something that happened to you on a trip. Use at least *five* of the verbs in the box in 1.

3. Listen to your partner's story and try to find which of the words in the box in 1 he or she used.

Something Went Wrong

Expressions of past time; *so, because*

VOCABULARY

1. Work in pairs. Put the words and phrases in the vocabulary box with the following travel situations. Some words can go with more than one situation.

a train journey   a boat journey   a plane flight
hotel accommodations

> airport   bed and breakfast   boarding pass   book
> business class   cabin   check in   check out
> connection   delay   departure   double room   fare
> ferry   harbor   lift   luggage   one way   passenger
> platform   reservation   round trip   schedule
> single room   terminal   ticket   take off

2. Think of two or three more words which go with each situation.

LISTENING AND SPEAKING

1. Look at these phrases taken from a story about a situation where something went wrong. Decide which travel situation in *Vocabulary* activity 1 the speaker, Bob, is describing. What do you think happened?

sat down on the tiny single bed	☐
knocked on the door	☐
slept in the car that night	☐
didn't have a reservation	☐
wanted to check out	☐
asked if he had a room	☐
left my suitcase in my car	☐
picked up a key from behind the desk	☐
was frightened by the man in the office	☐
showed me a very dusty room	☐

2. 🔊 Listen to Bob's story. Did you guess correctly in 1?

3. Number the phrases in 1 in the order you heard them.
🔊 Now listen to Bob's story again and check.

4. Have you ever been in a situation where something went wrong? Tell the class about it.

GRAMMAR

Expressions of past time

You can use these expressions of past time to say when something happened

last night   last Sunday   last week   last month   last year
yesterday   yesterday morning   yesterday afternoon
the day before yesterday
two days ago   three weeks ago   years ago   a long time ago
in 1985   from 1988 to 1997

So, because

You can join two sentences with so to describe a consequence.

The main hotel was full, so he went to a small motel.

You can join the same two sentences with because to describe a reason.

He went to a small motel because the main hotel was full.

---

1. Think of four or five important or memorable events in your life. Write down when they happened. Don't write down what happened.

five years ago   last year   three months ago...

2. Work in pairs. Show each other what you wrote in 1. Ask and say what happened.

What happened five years ago? I went to the United States.

3. Join the two parts of the sentence with *because*.

1. He didn't have a hotel reservation
2. He walked past the motel
3. He decided to leave
4. He locked himself in his car

a. the room was dirty and unpleasant.
b. there were no lights on.
c. he was so scared.
d. he didn't expect to stay there long.

1. He didn't have a hotel reservation because he didn't expect to stay there long.

4. Rewrite the sentences in 3 using *so*.

1. He didn't expect to stay there long, so he didn't have a hotel reservation.

WRITING

1. Write an opening sentence about what happened to Bob.

Bob arrived in a town at ten o'clock.

2. When you are ready, give your sentence to another student and you will receive an opening sentence from someone else. Read it, then write another sentence to continue the story.

Bob arrived in a town at ten o'clock.
He looked for a hotel.
He didn't have a reservation.
The main hotel was full.
He went down the road to a small motel.
The lights weren't on.
He walked past it.

Continue writing and receiving sentences until the story is finished.

3. Now write the story in full by joining the sentences with *and, but, so,* and *because*.

Bob arrived in a town at ten o'clock. He looked for a hotel, but he didn't have a reservation and the main hotel was full. So he went down the road to a small motel. Because the lights weren't on, he walked past it...

4. Write about a situation you have been in where something went wrong.

9 | *Family Life*

Possessive 's; possessive adjectives

VOCABULARY AND LISTENING

1. Look at the words in the vocabulary box. Put the words in pairs. Two words
have no pairs. Which ones are they?

> aunt boy boyfriend brother child cousin daughter father friend girl
> girlfriend grandfather grandmother husband man mother nephew niece
> parent sister son uncle wife woman

aunt - uncle...

2. 📼 Listen to Kathy from Buffalo, New York talking about her family.
Draw a line to show each person's relationship to her.

Pat   Ray   Kelly   Christine   Tony   Craig   Larry   Carol

mother   sister   father   grandmother   brother   aunt   husband   uncle

GRAMMAR

> **Possessive 's**
> **You add 's to singular nouns to show possession.**
> *Kathy's father = her father*   *Larry's wife = his wife*
> **You add s' to regular plurals.**
> *the parents' house = their house*   *the boys' mother = their mother*
> **You add 's to irregular plural nouns.**
> *the children's aunt = their aunt*   *the men's room = their room*
>
> **Possessive adjectives**
> **I - my   you - your   he - his   she - her   it - its   we - our   they - their**
> *Larry is **my** husband.*

1. Work in pairs. Use the information in *Vocabulary and Listening* activity 2 and
say who these people are. Use the possessive 's.

1. Kathy (Ray)	4. Craig (Carol)
2. Ray (Kelly)	5. Carol (Kathy)
3. Kelly (Craig)	6. Kathy (Larry)

1. Kathy is Ray's sister.

2. Rewrite the sentences in 1 using possessive adjectives.

1. Kathy is his sister.

Family Life

How close are you as a
family? We talked to
Kathy Finley from
Buffalo, New York about
her family life.

1. "We usually see each other at least once a month, maybe more often. We have lunch together on Sunday if we haven't got anything special to do. Usually my grandmother and my uncle and aunt are there too—we're quite a large family! Sometimes my brother and his girlfriend come over—they live nearby.

2. "There's no one we call the head of the family, although my father's advice and opinion are very important in any decisions we make. My uncle Tony is in fact older than my father, so I suppose he's the real head of the family. But we all try to discuss things together when we meet.

3. "In most families, it's a small family group who live in the same house, mother, father, and the children before they get married. But if one of the grandparents dies, the other sometimes sells their home and goes to live with their children.

4. "In the United States most children want to leave home when they graduate from high school or go to college. Of course, the problem is that apartments are so expensive to rent here, and so we have to live with our parents. I lived in Syracuse with my mother and father until I got married."

SOUNDS

1. 🔲 Listen and underline the /ə/ sound.

together   parent   suppose   opinion   advice
husband   woman

Now say the words out loud.

2. Look at this true sentence.

Larry is Kathy's husband.

🔲 Listen and correct the statements below with the true sentence. Stress the changed word each time.

1. Larry is Kathy's uncle.
2. Tony is Kathy's husband.
3. Larry is Carol's husband.
4. Larry is Kathy's brother.
5. Larry is Kelly's husband.
6. Craig is Kathy's husband.

*1. No, Larry is Kathy's **husband.***

READING AND SPEAKING

1. Read *Family Life* and match the questions with each paragraph. There is one extra question.

a. Who's the head of the family?
b. How often does the family get together?
c. How many people live in your house?
d. How long do people live with their parents?
e. How many people live in the same house?

2. Which paragraphs give specific information about Kathy's family? Which paragraphs give more general information?

3. Work in pairs. In your country, do you talk about your family to people you don't know? If so, answer the questions above with specific information about your family. If not, answer the questions above with general information about family life in your country.

10 *My Kind of Town*

Have (got); there is

VOCABULARY AND LISTENING

1. Look at the words in the box. Check (✓) the features or facilities that your hometown has.

> art gallery beach cathedral café factory market movie theater museum nightclub park port restaurant shrine stadium swimming pool temple theater university

2. 📼 Listen to Laura, an American teacher who lives in Taipei. Check (✓) the features or facilities in 1 that she mentions.

3. What does Laura like about living in Taipei? Write down three things.

📼 Listen again and check.

4. Work in pairs. Underline the adjectives in the box.

> architecture bad beautiful boring busy cheap climate cold crowded dangerous dirty entertainment excellent expensive food good interesting large medium-sized modern old safe safety stores size small traffic

Which adjectives can you use to describe the features and facilities of your hometown? Can you think of other adjectives to describe them?

5. 📼 Listen to six people talking about their hometowns. Each one is talking about a different aspect of their town. Put the number of the speaker by the aspect they are talking about.

architecture	☐	climate	☐	cost of living	☐
entertainment	☐	food	☐	public transportation	☐
safety	☐	traffic	☐	size	☐

GRAMMAR

> **Have (got) and *there is***
>
> You use *have* and *have got* when you talk about facilities, possessions, or relationship. You often use the contracted form with *have got*, but not with *have*.
>
> *I've got a small apartment.*   or   *I have a small apartment.*
> *Taipei's got fantastic museums.*   or   *Taipei has fantastic museums.*
>
> When you talk about facilities, you can also use *there is/are*. You often use the contracted form in speech.
>
> *There's a fantastic museum downtown.*
> *There are factories in the suburbs.*
>
> **Negative**
>
> *Laura doesn't have a big apartment.*   *Laura hasn't got a big apartment.*
> *I don't have much time. I haven't got much time.*
>
> **You don't usually use *have got* in the past.**

1. Rewrite these sentences with contractions where possible.

   1. The university has a park.

   2. There is a modern subway system.

   3. He has got a swimming pool.

   4. I have got tickets to the theater.

   5. Taipei has some beautiful temples.

   6. There is a great view from this window.

2. Work in pairs. Say what features and facilities your hometown has and doesn't have.

It has two soccer stadiums, but it doesn't have an art gallery.

WRITING

1. Read Laura's description of Taipei. Write down all the advantages and disadvantages of living in Taipei.

Advantages: people are polite and friendly, streets are clean...

Disadvantages: air is polluted, too many tourists...

2. Join two advantages or two disadvantages together using *and.*

*The people are polite and friendly, **and** the streets are clean.*

Then join an advantage and a disadvantage together with *but.* Make sure they are all features which can go together.

*Apartments are expensive, **but** food and clothes are quite cheap.*

3. Make a list of the advantages and disadvantages of living in your hometown.

Advantages	*Disadvantages*
a lot of good restaurants	*prices are high*
there's a beautiful beach	*there are no parks*

4. Write sentences joining advantages or disadvantages using *and.* Then write sentences joining an advantage with a disadvantage using *but.*

It has a lot of good restaurants, and there's a beautiful beach.

There's a beautiful beach, but there are no parks.

5. Write a short description of your hometown. Use Laura's description and the sentences you wrote in 4 to help you.

My Kind of Town

I love living in Taipei, because it's so interesting. It's a very energetic city, but people are polite and friendly, so it doesn't feel crowded or stressful. The air is quite polluted, but the streets are clean and the parks are well-kept. There are a lot of beautiful temples and shrines to visit, and it's got one of the best museums in the world, but sometimes there are too many tourists! Of course, Taipei has malls, fast-food places, and video games, but the city also has some beautiful old parts, and I love exploring those. Apartments are expensive here, and the prices in some stores are pretty high, but food and clothes are quite cheap. I have a great life here. It's my kind of town.

Fluency **2** *What Time Is It?*

Telling the time

LISTENING AND SPEAKING

1. Look at the following conversations. Can you guess what the missing words are?

1. JERRY What are you doing this evening?

KATE Not much.

JERRY Would you ____ to go to a movie?

KATE Sure. What's ____?

JERRY There's a new Quentin Tarantino movie that just came out...

KATE Great! What time does it ____?

JERRY Seven o'clock. Why don't we ____ here at a quarter after six?

KATE Make it six o'clock. The traffic is pretty bad at that time.

JERRY ____ o'clock, then. See you downstairs.

KATE OK. See you ____ .

2. LENNY What ____ does the plane ____?

DIANA Ten thirty.

LENNY And what time is it ____?

DIANA It's about nine fifteen.

LENNY How ____ does it ____ to get to the airport?

DIANA ____ half an hour.

LENNY Well, we ought to leave right ____, I guess. I don't want to ____ it.

DIANA Relax! We've got plenty of time.

2. [cassette icon] Listen and check your answers to 1.

3. Work in pairs and act out the conversations.

4. Use the conversations in 1 to act out a conversation in the following situations. Invent times and places. Change partners each time.

1. You'd like to go to concert.
2. You have an English class.
3. You have to catch a train.
4. You have a business appointment.

5. Work in pairs and read these statements. Which ones are true for your country?

	Your country	The United States
Most people get up at about seven o'clock in the morning.		
People generally start work at nine o'clock.		
There's usually a coffee break at eleven o'clock.		
You have to be on time for appointments.		
You can arrive late for meetings with friends.		
Lunch is usually at noon.		
It's common to spend time with co-workers after work.		
People don't usually work late.		
Dinner is usually at eight o'clock.		
Most people are in bed before midnight.		

6. [cassette icon] Listen to Bill and check (✓) the statements which are true for the United States.

7. Work in pairs. Try to remember what Bill said in detail.

[cassette icon] Now listen again and check.

FUNCTIONS

Telling the time

What time is it?	*(It's) one o'clock.*
What time do you have?	*Ten after two/Two ten.*
Can you tell me the time, please?	*Ten to three/Two fifty.*
Five (minutes) after three.	*Three oh five.*
A quarter after four.	*Four fifteen.*
Twenty after five.	*Five twenty.*
Half past six.	*Six thirty.*
Twenty-five to seven.	*Six thirty-five.*
Twenty to eight.	*Seven forty.*
A quarter to nine.	*Eight forty-five.*
Five to eleven	*Ten fifty-five.*
Twelve o'clock noon/midnight.	
It's nearly ten thirty.	*It's exactly seven fifteen.*
It's just after six.	*It's about five thirty.*

The twenty-four hour clock is only used for timetables in the United States.

1. Write the times in the functions box in clock form.

2. Look at these clocks and say what the time is.

3. 🔲 Listen to four dialogues and decide what the situation is.

at a train station	at an airport
a recorded phone message	at a business meeting
at a family breakfast	at a ball game

4. Work in pairs and write down the times you heard.

Dialogue 1: Ten thirty

🔲 Now listen again and check.

READING AND WRITING

1. Read these comments from people from around the world about attitudes toward time. Which ones are similar to attitudes you share? Which ones are very different?

"The business day begins at nine o'clock and finishes at five. But I often have to work longer hours, maybe until six or seven. I don't have much choice if I want to keep my job." **Judy, San Francisco**

"I eat when I'm hungry, not when the clock tells me to. But most people have mealtimes, like one o'clock for lunch and seven o'clock for dinner."
Steve, Des Moines

"The first thing that struck me in New York was that everyone was in a hurry." **Lee, Taipei**

"I try to arrive for my class on time, but I'm usually five or ten minutes late." **Carlos, Mexico City**

"Why sit around talking to people? I've got a business to run. Time is money." **Ken, New York**

"If I'm ten minutes late for an appointment, I always say I'm sorry. It's bad manners to be late."
Frances, London

"Not many people work late. It's a sign of bad organization."
Peter, Frankfurt

"We have lunch between three and four in the afternoon, then work for another three hours, and then dinner at ten o'clock at the earliest." **Ramon, Madrid**

"If the person I want to see is very important, I expect to wait a long time." **Ram, Nepal**

"We have a saying: Let's meet at four. If I'm not there at five, leave without me at six and I'll be there by seven." **Khalil, Morocco**

2. Work in pairs. Write sentences about the attitudes toward time which each statement shows. Compare it with your country.

Judy has to work pretty hard, and is prepared to stay late at work. In my country, people like to go home on time.

Progress Check 6–10

VOCABULARY

1. Work in pairs and make a *word chain*. Each word must be associated with the word immediately before it. Start like this:

hotel   front desk   reservation   double room   bed   breakfast

2. Some words go together to make a new word. Sometimes you write them as two words: *double room*, and sometimes as one word: *railroad*

Put a word from list A with a word from list B and make new words.

A round   hotel   first   boarding   air   suit   credit

B pass   reservation   class   case   trip
card   port

3. It is useful to write down new vocabulary under headings, such as *travel, towns, family*, etc. You can also use more personal or impressionistic categories, such as *words that sound nice*, or *words that are like words in my language*. Look at the vocabulary boxes in Lessons 6 – 10 again. Choose words which are useful to you and group them under headings of your choice in your *Wordbank*.

GRAMMAR

1. Write these regular verbs in the past simple tense.

ask   carry   change   continue   decide   enjoy   finish
happen   like   listen   live   look   open   play   start
stay   stop   talk   test   try   travel   visit   walk   watch

2. Write these irregular verbs in the past simple tense.

be   become   do   go   get   have   know   leave
make   put   run   see   sit   sleep   take   tell

3. Complete this conversation with *did, didn't, was, wasn't, were*, or *weren't*.

1. "___ you enjoy your vacation?"   "Yes, I ___ ."
2. "___ the weather good?"   "Yes, it ___ ."
3. "___ you go to the local museums?"
   "Yes, we ___ . They ___ very interesting."
4. "___ you send any postcards?"   "No, we ___ ."
5. "___ you buy anything?"
   "No, we ___ have any money."
6. "___ you happy with the hotel?"
   "Yes, we ___ ."

4. Correct the mistakes in these sentences and questions.

1. Last winter I buyed a new coat.
2. What did M. F. Barry invented?
3. Why did J. C. Fargo angry?
4. Who did tell you about the concert?
5. Most people not believed that the London Bridge was in Arizona.
6. Why he decided to go to the motel?

5. Complete these sentences with *so* or *because*.

1. I was very tired, ___ I went to bed.
2. He went to the motel ___ the hotel was full.
3. She lived with her parents ___ she couldn't afford to move out.
4. I wanted to learn English ___ I joined this class.
5. They went home ___ you weren't here.
6. The teacher was late _____ her car broke down.

6. Complete these sentences with *I, my, you, your, he, his, she, her, we, our, they*, or *their*.

1. I know ___ face. Is she famous?
2. We know them pretty well. ___ children go to the same school as ours.
3. Phil, this is ___ friend, Mary.
4. What do you do, Pete? What's ___ job?
5. I'll call you later. What's ___ telephone number?
6. That belongs to me. It's got ___ name on it.

SOUNDS

1. 🔊 Listen and say these words out loud.

<u>th</u>is <u>th</u>eater ca<u>th</u>edral <u>th</u>ink <u>th</u>ank you <u>th</u>ey

Is the underlined sound /ð/ or /θ/? Put the words in two columns.

2. 🔊 Listen and say these words out loud.

n<u>o</u>t kn<u>o</u>w l<u>o</u>ts b<u>oa</u>t ph<u>o</u>to vide<u>o</u> sh<u>o</u>p d<u>o</u>n't g<u>o</u> disc<u>o</u> <u>o</u>pera

Is the underlined sound /ɒ/ or /əʊ/? Put the words in two columns.

3. 🔊 Listen to the sentences. Put a check (✓) if you think Speaker B sounds friendly.

1. **A** Did you arrive late this morning?
   B No, I didn't.
2. **A** She didn't say hello.
   B Yes, she did.
3. **A** Did you give me your passport?
   B Yes, I did.
4. **A** Did they pay you for the tickets?
   B No, they didn't.

Now work in pairs and say the sentences out loud. Try to sound friendly.

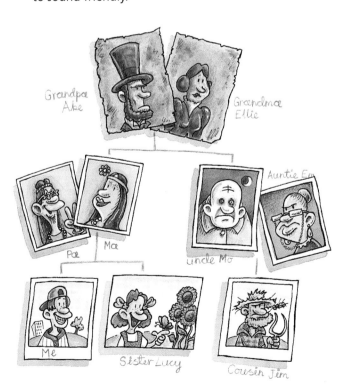

WRITING

1. You are going to write a story called *The Worst-Ever Baseball Team*. Look at the questions below and try to guess the answers. Write full answers to the questions. Leave a blank if there is any information that you don't know.

1. When was the New York Mets team started?
2. How did the City of New York welcome its new team?
3. Where did the parade go?
4. How many people were there?
5. What tune did the band play?
6. How many cars were there in the parade?
7. What did they throw into the crowd?
8. What happened in the first nine games?
9. How many games did they lose in the first season?
10. What record did the New York Mets set?

1. The New York Mets baseball team was started in...

2. Now turn to Communication Activity 14 on page 60 and read the story. Fill in the blanks in your version.

SPEAKING

1. Find someone in your class who:

- left home early this morning
- traveled by plane last month
- had a vacation three months ago
- walked to school/work ten days ago
- took a train last week   - rode on a bus yesterday
- stayed in a hotel last year   - went abroad in 1993

2. Draw your family tree, but include two "false" relatives who don't exist. Think of some interesting or unusual information about the homes of each relative and invent information for the two relatives who don't exist.

3. Work in pairs. Ask and answer questions about your families. Try to guess who the "false" relatives are.

11 *How Ambitious Are You?*

Verb patterns (2): *to* + infinitive; *going to* for intentions, *would like to* for ambitions

READING

1. How ambitious are you? Put a check (✓) by the ambitions you have. Do you have any other ambitions?

- run a marathon
- learn a foreign language
- travel around the world
- earn a lot of money
- write a novel
- become famous
- live abroad
- learn to fly

2. Read *How Ambitious Are You?* and answer the questions.

3. Turn to Communication Activity 5 on page 58 and find out how ambitious you are.

1. Your neighbor buys a new Mercedes. What do you say?
   a. I don't need an expensive car.
   b. One day I'm going to buy one, too.
   c. I'd like to let the air out of its tires.

2. Your boss leaves very suddenly. What do you think?
   a. They're going to give me his/her job.
   b. They're going to appoint someone else.
   c. They're going to say it's my fault.

3. Which ambition do you have?
   a. I'd like to be rich.
   b. I'd like to be famous.
   c. I'd like a drink.

4. You aren't happy with your job. What would you like?
   a. More responsibility.
   b. More money.
   c. More weekend.

5. What does your future hold for you?
   a. I'm going to be President.
   b. I'm going to be happy.
   c. I'm going to be late.

6. Which of these statements do you agree with?
   a. Every day, in every way, I'm getting better and better.
   b. Tomorrow is the first day of the rest of my life.
   c. If you don't succeed, try again. Then give up.

GRAMMAR

> ### Verb patterns (2)
>
> **You can put *to* + infinitive after many verbs.**
>
> *I **want to** leave now.* *He **decided to** drive to work.*
>
> *She's **learning** to fly.* *She **needs to** pass her exam.*
>
> ### Going to, would like to
>
> **You can use *going to* + infinitive to talk about future intentions or plans which are pretty certain.**
>
> *I'm studying medicine. **I'm going to** be a doctor. **I'm not going to** be an accountant.*
>
> **You can use *would like to* + infinitive to talk about ambitions, hopes, or preferences.**
>
> *I'**d like to** speak English fluently.*
> *I **wouldn't like to** run a marathon.*
>
> **Remember that *like* + *ing* means *enjoy*.**
>
> *I like learning English. = I enjoy learning English.*
>
> **For more information see Verb patterns (1) on page 9.**

1. Choose the correct verb pattern.

1. He got accepted to Harvard University. *He would like to/He is going to* study there.

2. She has her plane ticket, and *she'd like to/she's going to* go to Canada.

3. *He'd like to/He is going to* buy a new car, but it's too expensive.

4. *I'd like to/I'm going to* work in television but there aren't many jobs.

5. She enjoys her job. *She wouldn't like to/She isn't going to* change it.

6. He's got a new job with a foreign company. *He'd like to/He is going to* work abroad.

2. Work in pairs and talk about the ambitions you checked in *Reading* activity 1.

I'd like to run a marathon.

VOCABULARY AND WRITING

1. Match the verbs with the nouns in the box below.

> abroad   earn   a foreign language   learn   live   a marathon   money
> a novel   run   study   write

Can you think of other nouns which can go with the verbs?

2. Look at this passage about Hannah's ambition. Find out:

– what she'd like to do   – what she needs to do to achieve it
– why she'd like to do it   – what she's going to do

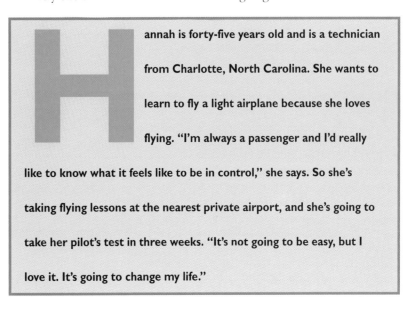

annah is forty-five years old and is a technician from Charlotte, North Carolina. She wants to learn to fly a light airplane because she loves flying. "I'm always a passenger and I'd really like to know what it feels like to be in control," she says. So she's taking flying lessons at the nearest private airport, and she's going to take her pilot's test in three weeks. "It's not going to be easy, but I love it. It's going to change my life."

3. Choose one ambition and make notes about why you'd like to do it.

earn a lot of money—buy a big house...

4. Now make notes about what you need to do to achieve it.

change my job, learn a foreign language...

5. Finally, make notes about what you're going to do to achieve your ambition.

look at job advertisements, go to night class...

6. Write a paragraph about your ambitions. Use the passage in 2 to help you. Join what you want to do and why with *because*.

I would like to earn a lot of money because I want to buy a big house.

Join what you need to do and what you're going to do with *so*.

I need to change my job, so I'm going to look at job advertisements.

***Will* for predictions**

VOCABULARY AND SOUNDS

1. Look at the words in the box and put them under two headings: *jobs* and *subjects*

accountant   actor   arithmetic
banker   biology   chemistry   dancer
doctor   economics   engineer
history   journalist   languages
physics   politician   secretary

2. Say the words in the box out loud. Which syllable is stressed? Put them in three lists.

First syllable   *actor*
Second syllable   *accountant*
Third syllable   *economics*

Listen and check.

3. Listen and say these words.

age   lesson   chemistry   economics
education   secretary   railroad
station   friend   vacation

Is the underlined sound /e/ or /eɪ/?

4. Work in pairs and look at the lists you made in 1. Which jobs do you need English for? Which subjects do you need English in order to study? Are there any other jobs and subjects you need English for?

LISTENING

1. Think about learning English in the future in your country. Which of these predictions do you agree with? Put a check (✓) if you agree and a cross (✗) if you disagree.

	You	Maggie	Greg	Your partner
Children will learn English from the age of six.				
There will be few adults who don't speak English.				
All classes at school will be in English.				
Everyone will need to learn about North American culture.				
Everyone will need English for their job.				
Everyone will learn English at home through television and computers.				
It will be more important to speak English than your own language.				

2. 📼 Listen to two English teachers, Maggie and Greg, talking about the statements. Put a check (✓) if the speaker agrees with the statements, a cross (✗) if he or she disagrees and put ? if it's not clear.

3. Work in pairs. Can you remember what Maggie and Greg said?
📼 Listen again and check.

GRAMMAR

Will

You use *will* to make a prediction or express an opinion about the future.
*Children **will learn** English from the age of six.*
*I think most people **will need** English for their job.*
*I'm sure everyone **will speak** some English.*

You form the future simple with *will* + infinitive. You often use the contracted form *'ll*.
*At the end of the course I**'ll speak** English fluently.*

Negatives
*There **won't be** traditional language classes in schools.*
*There definitely **won't be** many teachers.*

Questions
***Will** we **use** English at work?*
Short answers
*Yes, we **will**. No, we **won't**.*

1. Think about the end of your course. Make predictions about your level of English. Use *I will* or *I won't*.

1. speak English fluently
2. be able to read an American newspaper
3. be able to understand radio broadcasts
4. speak with a perfect American accent
5. be able to understand songs in English
6. know a lot of vocabulary

2. Look at these predictions about jobs and studying in the future. Do you agree or disagree? Write questions to ask another student.

1. computers – replace secretaries, accountants
2. journalists – disappear – because no newspapers
3. economics – the most important school subject
4. teaching by television – very common

1. Do you think computers will replace secretaries and accountants?

3. Now work in pairs and find out what your partner thinks.

Do you think computers will replace secretaries and accountants? No, I don't.

SPEAKING

1. In pairs, check your answers to *Listening* activity 2. Find out what your partner thinks and complete the *Your partner* column in the chart.

2. Find out what other people in your class think about the future of English.

Going to for plans and *will* for decisions; expressions of future time

LISTENING

1. You're going to hear Ryan, an American student, talking to a friend, Cathy about a trip he's going to make to South America. He's going to visit these places. Do you know which countries the places are in?

Places

The Amazon ☐   Machu Picchu ☐   Rio ☐

Santiago ☐   Lima ☐   Valparaiso ☐

2. 📼 Listen to the conversation and number the places in 1 as Ryan mentions them.

3. Work in pairs. Try to remember what Ryan plans to do in each place. Put the number of the place by what he's going to do there.

lie on the beach ☐   spend a week in the jungle ☐

visit the ruins ☐   take the cable car up the mountain ☐

do some sightseeing ☐   meet his girlfriend ☐

📼 Now listen again and check.

4. 📼 Listen to the rest of the conversation. Underline the verbs used.

CATHY Do you have a good guide book?

RYAN No, I don't. But *I'll get/I'm going to get* one. It's on my list of things to buy before I go.

CATHY Well, they say the best one is "South American Handbook".

RYAN Really? Well, *I'll get/I'm going to get* it when I go downtown.

CATHY Look, *I'll go/I'm going* downtown right now because I need to do some shopping. *I'll buy/I'm going to buy* it for you at the bookstore, if you want.

RYAN Really?

CATHY Yeah, sure.

RYAN Well, *I'll give/I'm going to give* you the money for it right now.

CATHY OK, and *I'll bring/I'm going to bring* it to your place tonight. Who knows, maybe *I'll borrow/I'm going to borrow* it from you someday.

RYAN OK. Thanks a lot.

GRAMMAR

> ### *Going to* for plans
> **You use *going to* to talk about things which are arranged or sure to happen.**
> *I'm **going to** visit South America.   I'm **going to** visit Lima.*
>
> **You use *going to* for decisions you made *before* the moment of speaking.**
> *I'm **going to** buy a guide book.*
>
> ### *Will* for decisions
> **You use *will* for decisions you make at the moment of speaking.**
> *I'll give you the money right now.*
>
> **You often use *will* for offers.**
>
> **You usually use the present continuous with *go* and *come*.**
> *He's **going** to South America.*   not   *He's **going to go** to South America.*
> *She's **coming** with us.*   not   *She's **going to come** with us.*
>
> ### Expressions of future time
> **You can use these expressions of future time to say when you are going to do things.**
>
> | ***tomorrow*** | *morning* | *afternoon* | *evening* |
> | ***next*** | *week* | *month* | *year* |
> | ***in*** | *two days* | *three months* | *five years* |

1. Does Ryan make his decisions before or at the moment of speaking to Cathy? Which verb form do you use to talk about decisions? Which one do you use to talk about plans?

2. Work in pairs and check your answers to *Listening* activity 3. Which things is Ryan sure he is going to do, and which things is he not sure will happen?

He's going to fly to Rio.
He'll probably take the cable car up the mountain.

3. Choose the correct verb form.

1. "I need a strong bag." "*I'm going to/I will* get you one."
2. I bought a good map, because *I'm going to/I will* go to South America.
3. "Where *will you/are you going to* stay?" "*We'll/we're going to* stay with friends, probably."
4. I need some fresh air. I think *I'm going to/I'll* take a walk in the park.

SPEAKING AND VOCABULARY

1. Work in groups of two or three. You're planning a trip somewhere. Decide where you'd like to go.

2. In your groups, look at the words in the box and decide which things you will need for the trip. Add three or four more things.

> aspirin backpack camera cash
> first aid kit food guide book
> map passport pocketknife purse
> razor scissors sleeping bag
> suitcase tent toothbrush
> toothpaste traveler's checks
> walkman wallet watch

3. Tell the others in your group which things you'll get.

I'll get the map.   OK, I'll buy some food.   Yes, and I'll bring my walkman.

4. Check who is going to get which things.

So, Ken is going to get the map, and Tanya is going to buy some food. Thanks for your help, Paco, but...

14 | *All That Jazz*

Prepositions of place; asking for and giving directions

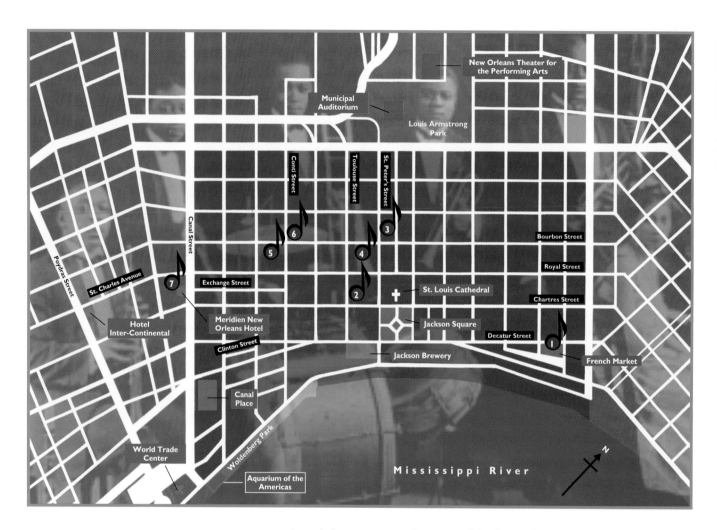

All That Jazz

Most jazz fans would agree that New Orleans is the place where jazz music was born, and every year hundreds of thousands of visitors come here to look for the real thing. The place to start, of course, is the atmospheric French Quarter, which is the heart of the city and home to many of the city's (and the country's) most famous jazz clubs.

A good place to start a walking tour of the Quarter's jazz clubs is at the **Palm Court Café**, next to the French Market on Decatur Street, where you can hear the traditional Dixieland style. From here, go south-west five blocks, and you'll see Jackson Square on the right. Walk through the Square towards St. Louis Cathedral, and then take a left on Chartres. Go down two blocks, and turn right on Toulouse. Find **Maxwell's Toulouse Cabaret** for more Dixieland.

From Maxwell's, walk up to Royal and turn right. Take the first left, and you're on St. Peter's, home of the world-famous **Preservation Hall**, a must-see for traditional jazz fans. From here you are half a block away from Bourbon Street, and you're at the **Maison Bourbon Nite Club**. Go three blocks, and you can find the **Famous Door Jazz Café**, and, on the corner of Bourbon and Conti, the **Famous Door**

One final stop before you return—tired but happy—to your hotel, is the **Jazz Meridien**, in the Meridien New Orleans Hotel on Canal Street. Continue down Bourbon until you get to Canal Street, then take a left. Go down two blocks, and you'll find it across from Exchange.

VOCABULARY AND READING

1. Work in pairs. Look at the words in the box and underline the adjectives.

> river real square concert hall cathedral famous
> hospital market traditional bus station theater
> happy park aquarium tired atmospheric

2. Look at the map of the French Quarter, in New Orleans. Can you see any of the features in the box in 1? What are the places called?

cathedral: St. Louis Cathedral...

3. Read *All That Jazz*, a guide to jazz clubs in New Orleans. As you read, find the names of the clubs numbered on the map and follow the route.

GRAMMAR

> ### Prepositions of place
>
> *St. Louis Cathedral is **across from** Jackson Square.*
> *The Aquarium of the Americas is **next to** Woldenberg Park.*
> *The Municipal Auditorium is **in** Louis Armstrong Park.*
> *The French Market is **between** Decatur Street and the Mississippi River.*
> *The Hotel Inter-Continental is **on the corner of** St. Charles Avenue and Poydras.*
> *Royal Street is **behind** St. Louis Cathedral.*
> *St. Louis Cathedral is **in front of** Royal Street.*
>
> **You often leave out words like *street* and *avenue* when giving directions.**
> *The bank is on First (Avenue) and Main (Street).*
>
> ### Asking for and giving directions
>
> *How do I get to...?* *Go straight (ahead)*
> *Go down/up...* *Go to the end of...*
> *Cross the street...* *Turn left/right on...*
> *It's on the left/right...* *It's at the intersection of First and Main.*
> *Take the first/second (turn on the) left/right.*
> *Go two/three blocks until you get to Main Street/the lights.*

1. Look at the map and say where these places are.

Jackson Brewery   the World Trade Center
Clinton Street   Canal Place
New Orleans Theater for the Performing Arts

2. Work in pairs. Write directions to get from Jackson Square to another place on the map but don't write the name of the place. Then give your directions to your partner and see if he or she can find it.

Turn left on Decatur and go three blocks...

SOUNDS

1. Say these words out loud.

<u>a</u>cross <u>a</u>gree <u>a</u>quarium <u>a</u>tmospheric <u>a</u>way
f<u>a</u>mous f<u>a</u>n fin<u>a</u>l h<u>a</u>lf h<u>a</u>ppy jazz pl<u>a</u>ce
st<u>a</u>rt   t<u>a</u>ke

Is the underlined sound /æ/, /ə/, /ɑː/, or /eɪ/? Put the words in four columns.

🔊 Listen and check.

2. Underline the stressed words in these questions.

1. Excuse me, how do I get to the bus station?
2. Pardon me, is there a bank near here?
3. Excuse me, could you tell me where the market is?
4. Pardon me, where's the nearest police station?

🔊 Listen and check.

SPEAKING

1. Work in pairs.

Student A: Think of a well-known place in the town where you are now. Imagine you are looking at it and describe where you are to Student B. Don't say what the place is.

Student B: Listen to Student A describing a well-known place in the town where you are now. Guess what the place is.

Change around when you're ready.

2. Work in pairs.

Student A: Turn to Communication Activity 4 on page 58.

Student B: Turn to Communication Activity 17 on page 60.

15 *An Apple a Day*

Expressions of quantity: countable and uncountable nouns, *some* and *any*, *much* and *many*

VOCABULARY

1. What sort of things do you eat, drink, or use in your cooking? Look at the words in the box and put them in four lists under these headings: *every day*, *twice a week*, *every week*, *on special occasions*, *never*.

apples bananas beef beer bread butter cabbage carrots cheese chicken coffee cookies eggs fish fruit grapes ham juice lamb lettuce meat milk oil onions oranges pasta peaches peas pork potatoes rice salad strawberries tea tomatoes vegetables water wine

Can you think of two or three more things to add to each list?

2. Work in pairs and compare your lists. Which of the things can you see in the photos?

3. Look at these words.

| bottle   can   cup   glass   loaf   package   piece   pound   slice |

a **bottle** of beer   a **can** of peaches   a **cup** of coffee
a **glass** of water   a **loaf** of bread   a **package** of cookies
a **piece** of cheese   a **pound** of potatoes   a **slice** of bread

Which other items in the vocabulary box can you use with these words?

GRAMMAR

> **Expressions of quantity: countable and uncountable nouns**
>
> **Countable nouns have both a singular and a plural form.**
> *an apple - two apples*   *a peach - two peaches*
>
> **Uncountable nouns do not usually have a plural form.**
> *bread   beef   butter   coffee   water*
>
> *Some* and *any*
> **You usually use *some* in affirmative sentences.**
> *I'd like an orange, two apples, **some** peaches, and **some** water.*
> **You usually use *any* in negative sentences and questions.**
> *We haven't got **any** butter.*   *Are there **any** eggs?*
>
> *Much* and *many*
> **You usually use *much* and *many* in negative sentences and questions. You use *many* with countable nouns.**
> *We don't have **many** carrots.*
> *How **many** eggs would you like?*
> **You use *much* with uncountable nouns.**
> *There isn't **much** cheese.   How **much** butter do you need?*

1. Look at the words in the vocabulary box again. Write *C* (countable) or *U* (uncountable) by them.

2. Complete the dialogue with *some, any, much,* or *many.*

A We need ___ water.
   How ___ bottles do we need?

B Two. And we don't have ___ fruit.
   Do you want to get ___ peaches?

A OK. Do we have ___ coffee?

B No, how ___ do we need?

A Just one pound.

   [cassette icon] Now listen and check.

LISTENING AND SPEAKING

1. Work in groups of three. You are going to hear Pat, who lives in San Francisco, and Karen, who lives in Hong Kong, talking about a typical breakfast, lunch, and dinner. First, make sure you understand these food items they mention:

cereal   pie   steamed dumplings   toast   sandwich
chowder   sub sandwich

2. *Student A*: Turn to Communication Activity 1 on page 58.

   Student B: Turn to Communication Activity 16 on page 60.

   Student C: Turn to Communication Activity 12 on page 59.

3. Now work together and complete the columns for Pat and Karen.

	Pat	Karen	You
Typical breakfast			
Typical lunch			
Typical dinner			

4. What do you have for a typical breakfast, lunch, and dinner? Complete the *You* column in the chart.

5. Compare the speakers' typical meals with your typical meals. Use these expressions.

a lot of/lots of   quite a lot of   a few/a little   not much/many   hardly any   not any

Pat eats a lot of fruit, and so do I. Karen eats hardly any sweet things, but I eat lots.

6. Find out what sort of things other people in your class eat, drink, or use in their cooking.

Seong-Hyun, do you drink tea?
Yes, I do.

Then find out how much they eat, drink, or use.

How much tea do you drink every day?
How many cups do you drink a day?

Fluency **3** *The Cost of Living*

Numbers and prices

VOCABULARY AND SPEAKING

Work in pairs. Which of the items in the box do you spend most of your money on?

> housing   food   entertainment   taxes
> transportation   gas   utilities   telephone
> medical   insurance   clothes   gifts

I spend most of my money on entertainment because I live with my parents.

Think about how much you spend on the items in the box.

Now go around and find out how much other people spend.

How much do you spend on food a month?

About two hundred dollars. How about you?

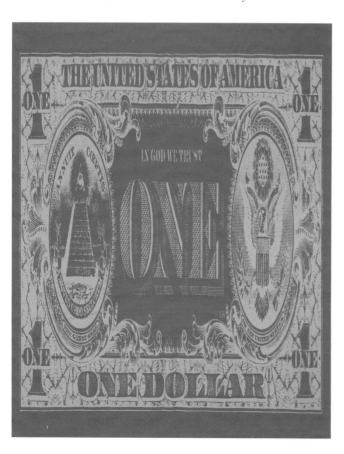

SPEAKING AND LISTENING

1. Read the dialogue. Where does it take place? Do you think you're likely to hear a similar conversation in your country?

CLERK Good morning, sir. What can I do for you?

MAN I'd like a pack of Marlboro, please.

CLERK Soft pack or box?

MAN Box, please.

CLERK Here, one pack of Marlboro. That's two-fifty. Do you want anything else?

MAN Oh, I need a gallon of milk.

CLERK The milk's behind you, in the refrigerator, sir.

MAN Right. And do you have today's paper?

CLERK Of course. That's fifty cents...and three twenty-nine for the milk, two fifty for the Marlboro. That's six twenty-nine altogether, sir.

MAN Here's ten dollars.

CLERK Out of ten? Here's your change—$3.71.

MAN Thanks.

CLERK You're welcome. Have a nice day.

2. 🔲 Listen and underline anything which is different from what you hear.

3. Work in pairs and check your answers to 2.

Now act out the dialogue you heard.

4. Work in pairs.

Student A: You're a sales clerk. Be ready to think of how much things cost.

Student B: You're doing some shopping. Think of three or four things you'd like to buy.

Now act out the dialogue. Use the dialogue in 1 to help you.

Change roles when you're ready.

40

FUNCTIONS

Numbers	
You write	**You say**
657	*Six hundred (and) fifty-seven*
12,501	*Twelve thousand, five hundred (and) one*
623,581	*Six hundred and twenty-three thousand, five hundred (and) eighty-one*
28%	*Twenty-eight percent*
10.4	*Ten point four*
6'3"	*Six (feet) three (inches) or: Six foot three*
¾	*Three quarters*
2⅞	*Two and seven eighths*
50' x 120'	*Fifty feet by one hundred and twenty feet*

Prices	
You write	**You say**
$1	*One dollar*
67¢	*Sixty-seven cents*
$8.99	*Eight dollars ninety-nine cents*
	Eight ninety-nine

1. How do you say these numbers?

505   a. Five hundred oh five
         b. Five hundred and five

478   a. Four hundred seven eight
         b. Four hundred and seventy-eight

3,563   a. three thousand, and five hundred sixty-three
         b. three thousand, five hundred and sixty-three

45,781   a. forty-five thousand, seven hundred and eighty-one
         b. forty-five thousand, seven hundred eighty and one

Now listen and check.

2. Say these words out loud. Underline the stressed syllable.

thirteen	thirty
fourteen	forty
seventeen	seventy
nineteen	ninety

thirteen dollars   fourteen feet   seventeen hours   nineteen miles

Listen and check.

3. **Listen and write down the numbers and prices you hear.**
Now say the numbers and prices out loud.

SPEAKING AND LISTENING 2

1. Work in groups of three. Look at the items in the chart. Say how much they cost in your country.

	Your country	Brazil	Malaysia
A gallon of milk			
A pound of fish			
A meal in a restaurant			
A bottle of wine			
A movie ticket			
A new car			
A newspaper			
A new television			
A house			
A gallon of gas			

1 gallon = 3.785 liters   1 lb. (pound) = 0.454 kg. (kilograms)

2. Work in groups of three.

Student A: Turn to Communication Activity 6 on page 58.
Student B: Turn to Communication Activity 13 on page 59.
Student C: Turn to Communication Activity 18 on page 60.

3. Work together and complete the chart.

4. Talk about prices in Brazil, Malaysia, and in your country. Are things more or less expensive?

Progress Check **11–15**

VOCABULARY

1. Word maps are a good way of remembering and organizing new vocabulary. Make a word map of your town or city.

good food

bars

my town

interesting people

nice buildings

cheap housing

2. Look at these words for jobs. Which come from verbs? Write the verb.

actor banker dancer journalist manager
musician politician teacher writer

actor - to act

Which ones come from other nouns? Write the nouns.

banker - a bank

You can make other words using a suffix. Look at these suffixes.

act**or** bank**er**

Underline all the suffixes in the words above. Words with these suffixes are often jobs.

3. Look at the vocabulary boxes in Lessons 11 – 15 again. Choose words which are useful to you and group them under headings of your choice in your *Wordbank*.

GRAMMAR

1. Write questions about Jane with *going to*.

1. be an accountant
2. live in the United States
3. start her own company
4. learn Portuguese
5. visit South America
6. start a new life

1. Is she going to be an accountant?

2. Write answers to the questions you wrote in 1.

1. be a doctor
2. move to Canada
3. work in a hospital
4. learn Spanish
5. travel around Spain
6. stay in contact with her old friends

1. Is Jane going to be an accountant?
No, she isn't. She's going to be a doctor.

3. You're going to start a new, exciting job tomorrow. Say what you are or aren't going to do.

– walk to work   – arrive early   – drink less coffee
– work hard   — be friendly   – stay late

4. Complete these sentences with *(be) going to* or *would like to*.

1. He's got his ticket and he ___ fly to São Paulo.
2. I ___ buy a car, but I don't have any money.
3. It ___ rain today.
4. We ___ go on a vacation but we're too busy.
5. He has his coat on and he ___ leave now.
6. We sold our apartment last week and we ___ live abroad.

5. Complete the sentences with *will* or *(be) going to*.

1. It's too early. Maybe ___ go back to bed.
2. He ___ fly to Rio next week.
3. She ___ have a baby next July.
4. "I'm so tired."   "I ___ take you home by car."
5. He has just gotten a job in Caracas, so he ___ move there.
6. Maybe we ___ have dinner in a restaurant.

6. Make predictions about the following.
Use *I think/perhaps/maybe + will*.

1. next weekend
2. your job
3. next vacation
4. your family
5. next year
6. your friends

7. Write sentences saying where these places are in your town. Use these prepositions:

at   on   across from   next to   in   between   behind   on the corner of   in front of

1. the post office
2. the bank
3. the library
4. the supermarket
5. the swimming pool
6. the movie theater
7. the stadium
8. the park

8. Write directions from where you are now to the following places.

1. the train station
2. the bus station
3. a gas station
4. the movie theater

9. Are these things countable or uncountable? Write *C* or *U*.

egg   money   orange juice apple   sugar   potato   butter rice   strawberry   cheese

10. Write questions using *How much ... do you have?* or *How many ... do you have?* and the words in 9.

How many eggs do you have?

How much money do you have?

11. Complete the sentences with *some* or *any*.

1. Do you have ___ oranges?
2. I'd like ___ wine, please.
3. I don't have ___ money with me.
4. Is there ___ water?
5. We have ___ chicken but we don't have ___ salad.
6. I'll get you ___ bread, if you want.

SOUNDS

1. Say these words out loud. Underline the /ə/ sound.

pizza   polite   police   America company   opera   performance potato   national

🔊 Now listen and check.

2. Say these words out loud.

<u>ch</u>arm   <u>ch</u>icken   politi<u>ci</u>an tradi<u>ti</u>onal   <u>ch</u>eese   <u>sh</u>e old-fa<u>sh</u>ioned   pea<u>ch</u>   fi<u>sh</u>

Is the underlined sound /tʃ/ or /ʃ/? Put the words in two columns.

🔊 Listen and check.

3. Look at this true sentence.

Joe is going to study math at the university.

🔊 Listen and answer the questions below. Change the stressed word each time.

1. Is Tim going to study math at the university?
2. Is Joe going to study physics at the university?
3. Is Joe going to study math at school?
4. Did Joe study math at the university?

1. No, **Joe** *is going to study math at the university.*

4. 🔊 Listen to these questions. Put a check (✓) if the speaker sounds polite.

1. How do I get to the station?
2. How do I get to the hospital?
3. Could you tell me where the city hall is?
4. Could you tell me where the bus station is?
5. Where's the post office?
6. Where's the river?

Now say the questions out loud. Try to sound polite.

SPEAKING

1. Work in pairs. One of the other pairs is coming for lunch. Decide:

– what dish you'll make
– where you'll have lunch.

2. Write a note to another pair. Say:

– where you're going to have lunch
– how to get there.

3. You need to buy the ingredients for the dish you chose in 1. Write each ingredient on a piece of paper. With your partner, discuss which ingredients you'll get.

A I'll get the tomatoes.

B And I'll buy some onions.

A OK. You're going to buy some onions, and I'm going to buy the tomatoes.

4. Give the pieces of paper with ingredients to your teacher, and you will receive some different ingredients. Go around asking other people if they have the ingredients that you're going to get and saying what you have.

Do you have any tomatoes?

Yes, I have./No, I haven't.

Give your ingredients to anyone who asks for them, even if you need them! The first pair to get all their ingredients is the winner.

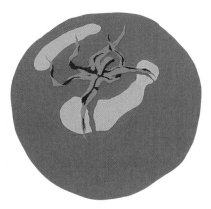

16 | *What's On?*

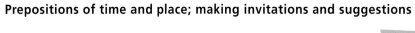

VOCABULARY

Look at the words in the box. Which words go under these headings: *What's on? Where?*

> ballet closing time club concert disco exhibition
> gallery game intermission movie movie theater
> museum musical opening hours opera
> opera house painting performance play row
> sculpture seat show stadium theater ticket

What's on?	*Where?*
ballet	*theater*
movie	*movie theater*

Now put the remaining words in a third column: *Related words.*

What's on?	*Where?*	*Related words*
ballet	*theater*	*ticket, row, seat*

LISTENING AND SPEAKING

1. Work in groups of three. You are going to hear people talking about typical entertainment in Japan and Argentina. Ken talks about *karaoke* in Japan, and Marybeth talks about *tango* in Argentina.

Student A: Turn to Communication Activity 2 on page 58.
Student B: Turn to Communication Activity 11 on page 59.
Student C: Turn to Communication Activity 15 on page 60.

2. How much do you know about karaoke and tango now? Work together and complete the chart.

	karaoke	tango
Type of entertainment		
Place of entertainment		
Performers		
Type of music		
Reasons why people enjoy it		

3. Talk about a typical type of entertainment in your country. Use the chart to help you.

GRAMMAR AND FUNCTIONS

Prepositions of time and place	
at	*the Civic Theater 8 P.M. the football game*
on	*Monday July 31st*
in	*June 1996 New York the United States*
to	*go to work go to the movie theater go to a party*

Making invitations and suggestions

Would you like to come to a movie?

How about com**ing** to a movie?

Let's go to a movie.

Accepting	**Refusing**
Sure. I'd love to.	*I'm sorry, I can't. I'm busy.*

1. Look at the prepositions of time and place in the grammar and functions box. Write the phrases in two columns: *time* and *place*.

2. Complete the rules about when we use *at*, *on*, or *in* to talk about time.

   1. You use ___ to talk about months and years.
   2. You use ___ to talk about days of the week and dates.
   3. You use ___ to talk about a point of time in the day (e.g. *eight o'clock*).

3. Complete these sentences with *at, in, on,* or *to*. Sometimes you can use more than one preposition. Is there a difference in meaning?

   1. The game starts ___ 3 P.M. ___ Saturday.
   2. ___ the Metropolitan Gallery ___ June and July there's a Van Gogh exhibition.
   3. I'd like to go ___ the opera when we're ___ Moscow.
   4. ___ Paris there's a World Cup football match ___ Saturday.
   5. I'm going ___ a party ___ June 20th.
   6. Would you like to come ___ the theater ___ New York ___ Sunday?

4. Make a list of what's on in your town at the moment. Go around the class inviting people to go out with you on different days. Accept or refuse their invitations, and try to fill up your appointment book.

   Would you like to come to the game on Friday?
   Yes, I'd love to!

   How about going to a movie on Saturday?
   I'm sorry, I'm busy. How about Sunday?

WRITING

1. Look at the formal invitation below.

Mr. and Mrs. Edward Perkins

invite

Felicity Brown and friend

to share in the marriage uniting their daughter

Joyce Elaine and Mr. Alexander Peter Kennison

on Saturday, the first of July at 4 o'clock in the afternoon

St. Anastasia Church, Seattle, WA

RSVP

Work in pairs. Invite your partner to go with you. Complete the letter.

475, East 9th

Tucson, Arizona

June 3

Dear _____

I've got an invitation from

_____

to join them on _____

for _____ . Would you

like to come? It starts at_____ .

Best wishes

_____

2. Give your partner your invitation. Now reply to his or her invitation. Use these phrases to help you.

Thank you for the invitation to...   I'd love to come.

Shall we meet at...   I'm afraid I'm busy.

17 | *Famous Faces*

Describing people

VOCABULARY

1. Work in pairs and look at the words in the box. Which are adjectives and which are nouns?

> attractive bald beard beautiful big black blond brown
> curly dark face fair glasses good-looking hair head kind
> long man medium-height middle-aged moustache nice old
> overweight pretty round short shy slim square straight
> tall teenager thin ugly woman young

Group any nouns and adjectives which often go together.

attractive face...

Which adjectives can you use to talk about the following?

– height   – age   – looks   – build   – character

2. Think of a famous person. Choose three or four words from the vocabulary box which you can use to describe his or her appearance.

Now tell your partner the name of your famous person. He or she must guess which words you chose.

My famous person is Mickey Mouse.
Did you choose short, dark, middle-aged?
Yes... and bald!

FUNCTIONS

> **Describing people**
> **Appearance**
> **You use *look like* to describe people's appearance.**
> ***What** does she **look like**?* She's tall and she has fair hair.
> She **looks like** a banker.
> ***Who** does he **look like**?* He **looks like** his father.
>
> **Character**
> **You use *be like* to describe people's character.**
> ***What's** he **like**?* He's nice.
> ***Who's** he **like**?* He's **like** his father.
>
> She's **kind of** short.   He's **about** twenty.   She's **about** five foot six.
> He's **very** tall.   He's **in** his **mid**-twenties.   She's **in** her **mid**-thirties.
> He's **really** handsome.   She's about thirty, **with** dark hair.

SPEAKING

1. Work in pairs. Choose someone in the pictures and describe him or her to your partner. Can they guess who you're describing?

2. Talk about what you imagine the people in the pictures are like. You can use the words in *Vocabulary* activity 1 to describe them. Which person do you think you'd like to meet? Explain why.

WRITING

1. You are going to the airport to meet someone who doesn't know you, and you're going to write a letter describing your appearance. First of all, make notes about these aspects of your appearance:

– age – height – looks – hair – build

age: mid-twenties   height: kind of tall

2. Now write sentences describing your appearance.

I'm in my mid-twenties. I'm kind of tall.

3. Then join the sentences using *and*.

I'm in my mid-twenties and I'm kind of tall.

4. Write a letter describing what you look like.

1. Complete the sentences with *like* if necessary.

1. What does she look ___? She looks ___ very kind.
2. Who's she ___? She's ___ her mother.
3. What's he ___? He's ___ wonderful!
4. Who does he look ___? He looks ___ his brother.

2. Match the questions and the answers.

1. How old is he?   a. Five foot eleven.
2. How tall is he?   b. Blond.
3. What color is his hair? c. He's kind of young, good-looking, and thin.
4. What does he look like? d. Twenty-one.

3. Look at the sentences in the functions box. Write four sentences describing people you know with *kind of*, *very*, and *really*.

My father is very old and really intelligent.

(Write your address here.)

(Write the date here.)

Dear Mr. Freeman

I am looking forward to meeting you at the airport next Monday. I will be there at ten o'clock and will wait for you at the gate.

(Describe your appearance.)

Yours sincerely
(Write your full name here.)

18 *Average Age*

Making comparisons (1): comparative and superlative adjectives

VOCABULARY

1. Work in pairs. Choose five words to describe yourself. Use a dictionary if necessary.

> calm careful cold confident
> cute fit funny imaginative
> intelligent interesting kind
> lazy nervous nice optimistic
> patient pessimistic polite quiet
> rude sad sensitive serious
> smart thoughtful tidy

Think of other words you can use.

honest, friendly...

Discuss your choice of words with your partner.

I think I'm usually optimistic. And I'm always polite!

Does he or she agree with you?

2. Think of three people you admire very much. They can be politicians, musicians, sports personalities, etc. or people you know personally. Choose the person you admire most and think of three adjectives to describe this person.

Then choose the second and third person you admire and think of three more adjectives for each person to explain why.

Now turn to Communication Activity 8 on page 59.

READING

1. Read *Average Age* and find things which are different from your experience or from the experience of people you know.

A v e r a g e   A g e

10 Ten is the year of the closest friendships—though not with the opposite sex. It is also the year when relationships with particular people or groups is strongest.

In the United States twenty is the average age for the first marriage for women, although probably only a third marry at this age because they want to; the others marry because of social pressure. The human brain is at its finest at twenty. **20**

30 For optimists thirty is one of the happiest ages, for pessimists it marks the end of feeling young. At this age you need to take a little more care with your body than when you were younger. Young people who enjoyed an all-night party at twenty will feel much worse the next day at thirty.

Forty is the year of the "middle-aged", although nobody who is forty wants to admit the fact. The body starts to get smaller at forty and continues to do so until you die. **40**

50 Fifty is an age when old friendships get closer and relationships with colleagues and relatives warmer. According to old proverbs, fifty is the age when you should be rich. People need to wear glasses and some food loses its strong taste.

Adapted from *The Book of Ages*, by Desmond Morris

2. Work in pairs. Which is the most surprising piece of information in the passage?

GRAMMAR

> **Making comparisons (1)**
> Comparative adjectives
> **You form the comparative of most adjectives by adding -er, -r, -ier, or more + adjective.**
> *kinder nicer lazier sadder more careful*
> *Fifty is an age when old friendships get **closer.***
>
> Superlative adjectives
> **You form the superlative of adjectives with -est, -st, -iest, or most + adjective.**
> *kindest nicest laziest saddest most careful*
> *For optimists thirty is one of the **happiest** ages.*
>
> **There are some irregular comparative and superlative forms.**
> *good better best   bad worse worst*

1. Look at the comparative and superlative adjectives in the grammar box. Write down the adjective they come from and the comparative and superlative forms.

kind   kinder   kindest

What's the rule for forming the comparative and superlative forms of short adjectives ending in -e, -y, a vowel + consonant?

What's the rule for forming the comparative and superlative forms of longer adjectives?

2. Make comparative and superlative adjectives from the following.

cold   imaginative   intelligent   healthy   tidy
beautiful   polite   patient   young   funny   nervous
warm   old

3. Work in groups of two or three. Talk about the best age for doing the following things.

– getting married   – buying a home   – having children
– leaving your parents' home   – going to college
– learning a foreign language   – leaving school
– learning to drive

I think it's best to get married at twenty-five.

SPEAKING

1. Choose a superlative adjectives you made in *Grammar* activity 2 to complete these questions about exceptional people, places, and things.

– Who is the ___ person you know?
– What is the ___ thing you own?
– What is the ___ time of the year?
– Where is the ___ place you know?
– What is the ___ country for a vacation?
– Who is the ___ person to be with at a party?

Who is the funniest person you know?

2. Work in groups of three or four. Ask and answer the questions you wrote in 1 about exceptional people, places, and things.

I think the funniest person I know is Eric.

49

19 Dressing Up

Making comparisons (2):
more than, less than, as...as

VOCABULARY

1. Look at these words for clothes. Which do you wear? Put the words in four lists under these headings: *always, often, sometimes, never.*

> blouse   coat   dress   hat   jacket   jeans   nylons
> pants   shirt   shoes   skirt   sneakers   socks   suit
> sweater   swimsuit   tie   T-shirt   underwear

always: underwear   often: jeans
sometimes:...

Think of other clothes you wear in winter, in summer, for work, and at home and add them to your lists.

2. Choose suitable adjectives from the list below to describe your own clothes. Add them to the four lists you made in 1.

> black   blue   brown   casual   formal   good
> green   gray   orange   pink   red   white   yellow

always: dark pants   often: good jeans
sometimes:...

3. Work in pairs. Ask and say what you always, often, sometimes, and never wear.

Do you often wear pants, Abdullah?
Yes. I usually wear dark pants.

READING

1. Read *Dressing Up*, which is about clothing in India, and find out if it says anything about:

– clothes for work
– traditional dress
– young people's fashions

Check your answers with another student.

Dressing Up

Traditional dress in India for women is the *sari* and for men the *achkan* suit. The *sari* has its own distinctive style depending on which part of India it comes from—every region has its own special colors, decoration, and style—and some are much more beautiful than others. The men wear their heavy and expensive *achkan* suits on formal occasions, but for less formal occasions they wear the *kurtha* suit, a long shirt and loose pants, which is not as heavy as the *achkan*. Indian people wear lighter colors as they grow older, and at funerals white is the usual color to wear.

Many people wear western-style clothes. For work they wear nice clothes, but not suits and ties. Women usually wear pants and blouses but not dresses. Young people are as casual as young people all over the world with their jeans and T-shirts.

2. Work in pairs. Ask and say what clothes people in your country wear. Talk about clothes for work, clothes at home, traditional dress, and young people's fashions.

Men wear suits for work. What do you wear?

GRAMMAR AND FUNCTIONS

> Making comparisons (2): *more than, less than, as...as*
> *Some are much **more** beautiful **than** others.*
> *They're **less** formal **than** they were.*
> *They're **as** casual **as** teenagers are all over the world.*
> *The kurtha is **not as** heavy **as** the achkan.*
> ***It's the same as** my country.*
> ***It's different from** my country.*

1. Complete these sentences with *as*, *than*, or *from*.

1. He's much smarter ___ I am.
2. She's ___ intelligent ___ he is.
3. Her clothes are different ___ mine.
4. She has the same shoes ___ I have.
5. Sandals are less common here ___ in Florida.
6. Kids are more casual ___ their parents.

2. Agree with these statements using *more* or *less* and the adjective in parentheses.

1. He's less casual than she is. (formal)
2. It's noisier now than it was. (quiet)
3. Clothes are cheaper here than at home. (expensive)
4. He's less optimistic than she is. (pessimistic)
5. It's easier to get good clothes here. (difficult)
6. He's less confident than she is. (nervous)

1. Yes, he's more formal than she is.

3. Write four sentences comparing what you wear and your appearance with other people. Use comparative adjectives.

I wear more colorful clothes than my father.

SOUNDS

1. 🔲 Listen to the sentences in *Grammar and Functions* activity 1. Notice that *than* is pronounced /ðən/, *as* is pronounced /əz/, and *from* is pronounced /frəm/.

Now say the sentences out loud.

2. 🔲 Listen to someone disagreeing with the statements in *Grammar and Functions* activity 2.

Now work in pairs and disagree with the statements. Stress *more* or *less*.

LISTENING AND SPEAKING

1. Read these statements. Decide if they are true or false for your country.

	My country	the United States
1. Nice clothes aren't expensive.		
2. Casual clothes are very expensive.		
3. People are very formal.		
4. Many people are kind of small.		
5. The quality of clothes design is good.		

2. 🔲 Listen to Don from San Francisco talking about clothing. Does he think the statements in 1 are true or false?

3. Work in pairs and answer the questions.

In your country...

– are nice clothes cheaper or more expensive?
– are casual clothes cheaper or more expensive?
– are people more formal or more casual?
– are people smaller or larger than Americans?
– is the quality of clothes design better or worse?

In my country nice clothes are more expensive.

20 *Memorable Journeys*

Talking about journey time, distance, speed, and prices

VOCABULARY AND SOUNDS

1. Work in pairs and look at the photo. Use these words to describe what you can see.

arrive border cost desert
distance drive driver gallon
gas station get highway hill
leave mile motel mountain
move home passenger
police patrol reach set out
speed limit ticket truck turn off

2. Say these numbers out loud.

346 678 2,345 18,664 24,589
123,456 202 54,566 3,481 407
10,020

🔲 Now listen and check.

LISTENING

1. 🔲 Listen to Sarah talking about a memorable journey she made across the United States. As you listen, look at the vocabulary box again and check (✓) the words you hear.

2. Check (✓) the information you heard.

Journey time	9 days	19 days	90 days
Distance	250 miles	2,050 miles	2,500 miles
Price of gas	$1 a gallon	$1.40 a gallon	60 cents a gallon
Speed limit	50 miles an hour	55 miles an hour	70 miles an hour
Price of motel rooms	$20 to $35 per person	$25 to $40 per person	$30 to $50 per person

🔲 Now listen again and check. Would you like to make a journey like Sarah's?

GRAMMAR

Talking about journey time, distance, speed, and prices	
Journey time	
How long does it take **by** *car*	*(It takes) nine days.*
How long does it take **by** *train?*	*Five hours.*
How long does it take **on** *foot?*	*It's a five-minute walk/drive/flight/journey.*
Distance	
How far is it?	*It's 2,500 miles **away**.*
How far is your school from your home?	*Ten miles.*
Speed	
How fast can you drive?	*Fifty-five miles **per** hour. (mph)*
	*Fifty-five miles **an** hour.*
Prices	
How much is gas?	*(It's) $2 **a** gallon.*
How much does gas cost?	*(It costs) $2 **a** gallon.*
How much are hotel rooms?	*$25 **per** person **per** night.*
How much do hotel rooms cost?	

1. Work in pairs and check your answers to *Listening* activity 2.

2. Imagine these are the correct answers to questions about your country. Write the questions using *How long* or *How far.*

1. An hour.
2. 500 miles.
3. Half an hour.
4. 20 miles.
5. Two weeks.
6. It's three miles away.
7. Ten hours.
8. It's a ten-minute drive.

1. An hour.   How long does it take to get from Buenos Aires to Cordoba by plane?

2. 500 miles.   How far is it from Yokohama to Hakodate?

3. Write six questions about journey time, distance, speed, and prices in your country.

How fast can you drive in town?

Now work in pairs and ask and answer questions about journey time, distance, speed, and prices.

SPEAKING

1. Think about a memorable journey by car across your country. What is the best route to take?

Now work in pairs and talk about your journeys.

2. Look at some more information about the United States.

Tallest building	Sears Tower, Chicago, 1,453 ft.
Highest mountain	Mount McKinley, Alaska, 20,321 ft.
Longest river	Mississippi River, 3,741 miles
Largest lake	Lake Superior, 31,820 square miles
Biggest city	New York City, population 7.5 million
Hottest place	Death Valley, average temperature 122°F in July
Coldest region	Alaska, average temperatures 10°F in January

Write two questions for each piece of information

What's the tallest building?   How tall is it?

3. Think about answers to the questions about your country. It doesn't matter if you don't know the exact figures.

Now work in pairs and ask and answer questions about your country.

Igor, what's the largest lake in Venezuela?
It's Maracaibo.

How large is it?
It's more than 21,000 sq. km.

Fluency **4** Special Occasions

Saying dates; saying the right thing

VOCABULARY AND READING

1. Write down the months of the year in the right order.

April   August
February   Friday
December   January
July   June
March   May
Monday   November
October   Saturday
September   Sunday
Thursday   Tuesday
Wednesday

January...

2. Write down the days of the week.

Sunday...

3. Work in pairs. Do any of the days of the week or months of the year have any special association for you?

4. Read this passage about days of the week. Do the days of the week have similar associations in your country?

Different days have different activities associated with them. In the United States, many people joke about disliking Monday morning, when the working week begins. Friday is payday for many non-professional workers. It is also the last working day before the weekend, and people often feel very happy when Friday comes. People may go out for a meal or a drink after work on Friday, to say "TGIF" (Thank God it's Friday!). Saturday is a busy shopping day. Most people do not work on Saturday. It is also a day for doing jobs at home, such as cleaning the car. In the afternoon there are sports events like ball games, and in the evening people often go out for a meal or to a friend's house for dinner. Sunday is the day when many people go to church. The main church service is usually in the morning. Other people sleep in, staying in bed late and reading a Sunday paper, which is larger than the daily one. Many people follow the custom of having brunch, which is breakfast and lunch together. People may visit friends or relatives, or go out somewhere. In most small towns, the stores are usually closed on Sundays.

5. Work in pairs. What traditional activities do you associate with the days of the week in your country?

LISTENING AND SPEAKING

1. Put this dialogue in the right order.

A   Socks! What a fantastic present! Anything else?
B   Yes, I'm going for a walk in the park.
C   And are you going to do anything to celebrate?
D   It's my birthday today.
E   You sure are celebrating in style. Have a wonderful time.
F   Thank you.
G   Congratulations! Did you get any presents?
H   Yes, I got a neat pair of socks.
I   Yes, I also got some nice handkerchiefs. They're just what I've always wanted.

2. 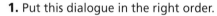 Listen and check your answer to 1.

3. Work in pairs. Act out the dialogue in 1. You can change any details you like.

FUNCTIONS

> **Saying dates**
>
> | You write | You say |
> |---|---|
> | *July 1, 1987* | *July first, nineteen eighty-seven* |
> | *Thursday, October 23* | *Thursday, October twenty-third* |
> | *1/15/96* | *January fifteenth, nineteen ninety-six* |
> | *Friday, June 20, 2002* | *Friday, June twentieth, two thousand and two* |
>
> **Saying the right thing**
>
> | | | |
> |---|---|---|
> | *Happy birthday* | *Merry Christmas* | *Congratulations* |
> | *Happy New Year* | *Happy Mother's Day* | *Happy Easter* |
> | *Happy Thanksgiving* | *Happy Halloween* | |

1. Write these ordinal numbers in full.

11th   23rd   1st   15th   2nd   9th   31st   17th

2. Write the following dates as you say them.

1. 1/13/77   2. April 1, 1996   3. May 3, 1980
4. Friday, January 1, 2010   5. February 6, 1999   6. October 24, 2001

3. Say when these dates are in the United States or in your country.

Christmas Day   New Year's Eve   New Year's Day   Halloween
Independence Day   your birthday

4. What do you say on the days in 3?

Merry Christmas

5. Are there any other special days on your calendar? Say what date they are.

Mayday   May first

LISTENING

1. You're going to hear Judy talking about holidays in the United States. Work in groups of three.

Student A: Turn to Communication Activity 7 on page 58.

Student B: Turn to Communication Activity 10 on page 59.

Student C: Turn to Communication Activity 19 on page 60.

	Date	Reasons	Customs
Valentine's Day			
Mother's Day			
Independence Day			
Labor Day			
Thanksgiving Day			

2. Work together and complete the chart in as much detail as possible.

🔊 Now listen again and check.

3. Choose some important holidays in your country and talk about the date, the reason, and the customs.

In my country we celebrate Girls' Day...

Progress Check ◯16–20

VOCABULARY

1. Look at these international words.

> pizza hamburger sushi disco rock television
> football restaurant concert tennis theater movie
> ballet opera jazz stadium museum video

Put them in these groups: *food, sports, places, types of entertainment, music*.

If you know any more international words, add them to your groups of words.

2. Look at the endings used for these adjectives.

friend**ly** gener**ous** act**ive** dynam**ic** confid**ent**
thought**ful** temperament**al** nois**y** cap**able**

Now look at the adjectives in Lesson 18 again. Are there any with similar endings? Words with these endings are often adjectives.

3. Some words are used either for men or for women, but not both. Put a cross (✗) by the sentences which sound odd.

1. He's got a really pretty face.
2. She bought some black nylons yesterday.
3. He wears a white blouse to the office.
4. She's a very handsome little girl.
5. He's got a warm nightgown for winter nights.
6. She has two pairs of blue jeans.

4. Decide if these items of clothing are usually worn by men or women, or both.

skirt bikini bra panties underpants nylons
boots swimsuit shirt shorts jacket sandals
pyjamas boxers

5. Look at the vocabulary boxes in Lessons 16 – 20 again. Choose words which are useful to you and group them under headings of your choice in your *Wordbank*.

GRAMMAR

1. Complete these sentences with *in, at,* or *on*.

1. The football season starts ___ August and finishes ___ January.
2. The ballet is ___ the Apollo Theater.
3. It's ___ Monday June 22 ___ 7:30 P.M.
4. The game is ___ 7:15 P.M. ___ Saturday.
5. The Olympic Games ___ 1996 were ___ Atlanta ___ the United States.
6. The movie starts ___ 3 P.M. ___ Saturday.

2. Complete these sentences with *to* or *at*.

1. I like going ___ the theater.
2. I'm working ___ home tomorrow.
3. Let's meet ___ the movie theater.
4. The football game is ___ the main stadium.
5. Would you like to take us ___ the museum?
6. Let's walk ___ the swimming pool.

3. Write questions about Frank.

Ask about:

family likeness   age   height   color of hair   color of eyes   looks

4. Write sentences saying what Frank looks like.

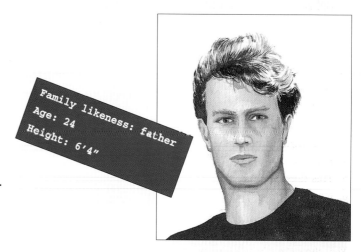

Family likeness: father
Age: 24
Height: 6′4″

56

5. Write sentences about what you look like. Use the questions you wrote in 3 to help you.

6. Choose the best words and complete the sentences.

1. She's got a very ___ face.
   a. curly b. tall c. pleasant.

2. He's got no hair. He's completely ___ .
   a. bald b. fair c. gray

3. He has a ___ gray beard.
   a. round b. long c. square

4. She's over six foot. She's really ___ .
   a. short b. honest c. tall

5. He works as a model. He's very ___ .
   a. good-looking b. careless c. bossy

6. It's cold today. I'll wear a ___ .
   a. swimsuit b. T-shirt c. coat

7. Write the comparative and superlative forms of these adjectives.

big calm careful confident cute friendly
generous imaginative informal lazy nervous
quiet small smart thoughtful tidy warm

8. Disagree with these statements. Use the adjective in parentheses.

1. Clothes are cheaper than food. (expensive)
2. Mike is taller than Phil. (short)
3. Canada is hotter than Brazil. (cold)
4. It's easier to buy nice clothes in the winter. (difficult)
5. Kate is younger than Frank. (old)
6. The North Americans are more formal than the South Americans. (casual)
7. Pete is more polite than Jack. (rude)
8. Bill is lazier than Joe.(hard-working)

1. No, they aren't. They're more expensive.

9. Agree with these statements using the superlative form of the adjective.

1. She's very kind.
2. It's a very beautiful town.
3. He's very polite.
4. She's very short.
5. This dress is very expensive.
6. It's a very powerful car.
7. He's extremely handsome.
8. She's very sensitive.

Yes, she's the kindest person I know.

10. Complete the dialogues.

A How ___ is it to the nearest gas station?
B It's fifty miles ___ .

A How ___ does it take ___ car?
B It's ___ five-minute drive.

A How long does it ___ to walk?
B It's thirty minutes ___ foot.

A How ___ is a ticket to Chicago?
B It ___ $246.

SOUNDS

1. Say these words out loud.

b<u>lue</u> g<u>oo</u>d b<u>oo</u>k sh<u>oe</u> b<u>oo</u>t s<u>ui</u>t m<u>o</u>ve t<u>oo</u>k c<u>oo</u>k

Is the underlined sound /ʊ/ or /uː/? Put the words in two columns.

Listen and check.

2. Say these words out loud. Underline the /dʒ/ sound.

geography journalist soldier engineer teenager job manager

Now listen and check.

3. Put these sentences in the correct order and make a dialogue.

a. Well, thanks anyway.
b. Sorry. This is the largest size we have.
c. Can I help you?
d. It's too small. Do you have it in a bigger size?
e. Yes, I'm looking for a sweater.
f. How about this one? It looks great on you.

Listen and check. Do you think the speakers sound polite and friendly?

Now work in pairs and say the sentences out loud. Try to sound polite and friendly.

SPEAKING AND WRITING

Work in pairs. You're going to recreate a story called *The Phantom of the Opera and the Empty Seat*.

Student A: Turn to Communication Activity 9 on page 59.

Student B: Turn to Communication Activity 3 on page 58.

Communication Activities

1. *Lesson 15*
Listening and Speaking, activity 2

Student A: 🔲 Listen and find out what Karen has for breakfast and what Pat has for lunch.

When the recording stops, turn back to page 39.

2. *Lesson 16*
Listening and Speaking, activity 1

Student A: 🔲 Listen and find out what type of entertainment karaoke is, and what type of music they play. Find out where they perform tango and the reasons why people enjoy it.

When the recording stops, turn back to page 44.

3. *Progress Check 16 - 20*
Speaking and Writing

Student B: Dictate these sentences to Student A in turn. Write down the sentences Student A dictates.

1. _____

   _____

2. So when a man finally got tickets he was surprised to find an empty seat between him and the next person, a woman dressed in black.

3. _____

   _____

4. The woman replied, "Yes, we bought them some months ago but then my husband died."

5. _____

   _____

6. The woman said, "Well, they're all at the funeral."

4. *Lesson 14*
Speaking, activity 2

Student A: Give *Student B* directions from places in column 1 to places in column 2. Tell *Student B* where you start from but not where you're going to.

1.	**2.**
Municipal Auditorium	French Market
Woldenburg Park	Jazz Meridien
Jackson Square	Louis Armstrong Park

Change around when you're ready.

5. *Lesson 11*
Reading, activity 3

Mostly "a"
You're extremely ambitious. You're never satisfied with your life and you're always trying to improve things. Try to relax and take things easy!

Mostly "b"
You're fairly ambitious. You are very aware that life has much to offer, but you don't feel you can achieve very much. Keep trying but don't make yourself unhappy.

Mostly "c"
You're so unambitious, you don't even know the meaning of the word. Look it up in a dictionary, if you can be bothered.

6. *Fluency 3*
Speaking and Listening 2, activity 2

Student A: 🔲 Listen and find out how much the following things cost:

Brazil: a gallon of milk, a meal in a restaurant, a new car, a house
Malaysia: a pound of fish, a bottle of wine, a newspaper, a gallon of gas

7. *Fluency 4*
Listening, activity 1

Student A: 🔲 Listen and find the answers to these questions:

1. What date is Valentine's Day and Labor Day?

2. What is the reason for Independence Day?

3. What customs are there on Mother's Day and Thanksgiving Day?

8. *Lesson 18*
Vocabulary, activity 2

The words you chose to describe the first person show the kind of person you'd like to be. The words you chose for the second person show how you think other people see you. The words you use to describe the third person show the real you, your true character!

9. *Progress Check 16 - 20*
Speaking and Writing

Student A: Dictate these sentences to *Student B* in turn. Write down the sentences *Student B* dictates.

1. *The Phantom of the Opera* was one of Broadway's most popular musicals and it was difficult to reserve seats.

2. _____
   _____

3. He said, "It took me a long time to get tickets for this show."

4. _____
   _____

5. The man said, "I'm so sorry. But why didn't you ask a friend or a relative to come with you?"

6. _____
   _____

10. *Fluency 4*
Listening, activity 1

Student B: 🔊 Listen and find the answers to these questions:

1. What date is Independence Day and Thanksgiving Day?
2. What is the reason for Valentine's Day and Mother's Day?
3. What customs are there on Labor Day?

11. *Lesson 16*
Listening and Speaking, activity 1

Student B: 🔊 Listen and find out where they perform karaoke and the reasons why people enjoy it. Find out who performs tango.

When the recording stops, turn back to page 44.

12. *Lesson 15*
Listening and Speaking, activity 2

Student C: 🔊 Listen and find out what Pat has for breakfast and what Karen has for dinner.

When the recording stops, turn back to page 39.

13. *Fluency 3*
Speaking and Listening 2, activity 2

Student B: 🔊 Listen and find out how much the following things cost:

Brazil: a pound of fish, a bottle of wine, a newspaper, a gallon of gas
Malaysia: a bus ticket, a movie ticket, a new television

14. *Progress Check 6 - 10*
Writing, activity 2

Read the passage and complete your version of the story

> **The Worst-Ever Baseball Team**
>
> On April 13, 1962, the City of New York welcomed its new baseball team, the New York Mets. Forty thousand people watched as the team paraded down Broadway and the band played "Hey, Look Me Over." The team rode in fourteen rainbow-colored cars. As they moved, they threw 10,000 plastic baseballs and bats into the crowd.
>
> However, the team did not play very well. They lost their first nine games, which was almost a baseball record. At the end of the season, they had lost 120 games, which was more than any other team in the history of baseball!
>
> Adapted from *Cannibals in the Cafeteria*, by Stephen Pile

15. *Lesson 16*
Listening and Speaking, activity 1

Student C: 🔲 Listen and find out who performs karaoke. Find out what type of entertainment tango is and what type of music they play.

When the recording stops, turn back to page 44.

16. *Lesson 15*
Listening and Speaking, activity 2

Student B: 🔲 Listen and find out what Karen has for lunch and what Pat has for dinner.

When the recording stops, turn back to page 39.

17. *Lesson 14*
Speaking, activity 2

Student B: Give *Student A* directions from places in column 1 to places in column 2. Tell *Student A* where you start from but not where you're going to.

1.	**2.**
Palm Court Café	Aquarium of the Americas
Preservation Hall	World Trade Center
Jackson Brewery	Famous Door

Change around when you're ready.

18. *Fluency 3*
Speaking and Listening 2, activity 2

Student C: 🔲 Listen and find out how much the following things cost:

Brazil: a bus ticket, a movie ticket, a new television
Malaysia: a gallon of milk, a meal in a restaurant, a new car, a house

19. *Fluency 4*
Listening, activity 1

Student C: 🔲 Listen and find the answers to these questions:

1. What date is Mother's Day?
2. What is the reason for Thanksgiving Day and Labor Day?
3. What customs are there on Independence Day and Valentine's Day?

Grammar Review

CONTENTS

Present simple

Form

You use the contracted form in spoken and informal written English.

Be

Affirmative	Negative
I'm (I am)	I'm not (am not)
you	you
we 're (are)	we aren't (are not)
they	they
he	he
she 's (is)	she isn't (is not)
it	it

Questions	Short answers
Am I	Yes, I am.
	No, I'm not.
Are you/we/they?	Yes, you/we/they are.
	No, you/we/they're not.
Is he/she/it?	Yes, he/she/it is.
	No, he/she/it isn't.

Have

Affirmative	Negative
I	I
you have	you haven't (have not)
we	we
they	they
he	he
she has	she hasn't (has not)
it	it

Questions	Short answers
Have I/you/we/they?	Yes, I/you/we/they have.
	No, I/you/we/they haven't.
Has he/she/it?	Yes, he/she/it has.
	No, he/she/it hasn't.

Regular verbs

Affirmative	Negative
I	I
you work	you don't (do not) work
we	we
they	they
he	he
she works	she doesn't (does not) work
it	it

Questions	Short answers
Do I/you/we/they work?	Yes, I/you/we/they do.
	No, I/you/we/they don't.
Does he/she/it work?	Yes, he/she/it does.
	No, he/she/it doesn't.

Question words with *is/are*
What 's your name? Where are your parents?

Question words with *does/do*
What do you do? Where does he live?

Present simple: third person singular
(See Lesson 2.)

You add *-s* to most verbs.
takes, gets

You add *-es* to *do*, go, and verbs ending in *-ch*, *-ss-*, *-sh*, and *-x*.
goes, does, watches, finishes

You add *-ies* to verbs ending in *-y*.
carries, tries

Use

You use the present simple:

- to talk about customs and habits. (See Lesson 1.)
  In my country men go to restaurants on their own.

- to talk about routine activities. (See Lesson 2.)
  He gets up at 6:30.

- to talk about a habit. (See Lesson 5.)
  He smokes twenty cigarettes a day.

- to talk about a personal characteristic. (See Lesson 5.)
  She plays the piano.

- to talk about a general truth. (See Lesson 5.)
  You change money in a bank.

Present continuous

Form

You form the present continuous with *be* + present participle (*-ing*). You use the contracted form in spoken and informal written English.

Affirmative	Negative
I'm (am) working	I'm not (am not) working
you	you
we 're (are) working	we aren't (are not) working
they	they
he	he
she 's (is) working	she isn't (is not) working
it	it

Questions	Short answers
Am I working?	Yes, I am.
	No, I'm not.
Are you/we/they working?	Yes, you/we/they are.
	No, you/we/they aren't.
Is he/she/it working?	Yes, he/she/it is.
	No, he/she/it isn't.

Question words
What are you doing? Why are you laughing?

Present participle *(-ing)* endings

You form the present participle of most verbs by adding *-ing*.
go - going, visit – visiting

You add *-ing* to verbs ending in *-e*.
make- making, have- having

You double the final consonant of verbs of one syllable ending in a vowel and a consonant, and add *-ing*.
get- getting, shop- shopping

You add *-ing* to verbs ending in a vowel and *-y* or *-w*.
draw- drawing, play- playing

You don't usually use these verbs in the continuous form.
believe   feel   hear   know   like   see   smell sound   taste   think   understand   want

Use

You use the present continuous to say what is happening now or around now. There is an idea that the action or state is temporary. (See Lesson 5.)
It's raining. I'm learning English.

Past simple

Form
You use the contracted form in spoken and informal written English.

Be

Affirmative	Negative
I	I
he was	he wasn't (was not)
she	she
it	it
you	you
we were	we weren't (were not)
they	they

Have

Affirmative	Negative
I	I
you	you
we	we
they had	they didn't (did not) have
he	he
she	she
it	it

Regular verbs

Affirmative	Negative
I	I
you	you
we	we
they worked	they didn't work
he	he
she	she
it	it

Questions	Short answers
Did I/you/we/they work?	Yes, I/you/we/they did.
he/she/it	he/she/it
	No, I/you/we/they didn't.
	he/she/it

Question words
What did you do? Why did you leave?

Past simple endings

You add *-ed* to most regular verbs.
walk- walked, watch- watched

You add *-d* to verbs ending in *-e*.
close- closed, continue- continued

You double the consonant and add *-ed* to verbs ending in a vowel and a consonant.
stop- stopped, plan- planned

You drop the *-y* and add *-ied* to verbs ending in *-y*.
study- studied, try- tried

You add —*ed* to verbs ending in a vowel + *-y*.
play- played, annoy- annoyed

Pronunciation of past simple endings

/t/ *finished, liked, walked*
/d/ *continued, lived, stayed*
/ɪd/ *decided, started, visited*

Expressions of past time
(See Lesson 8.)

yesterday	*the day before yesterday*	*last weekend*
last night	*last month*	*last year*

Use
You use the past simple:

● to talk about a past action or event that is finished.
(See Lessons 6, 7, and 8.)
He shipped it over from the River Thames.

Future simple (*will*)

Form

You form the future simple with *will* + infinitive. You use the contracted form in spoken and informal written English.

Affirmative	Negative
I	I
you	you
we	we
they 'll (will) work	they won't (will not) work
he	he
she	she
it	it

Questions	Short answers
Will I/you/we/they work?	Yes, I/you/we/they will.
he/she/it/	he/she/it/
	No, I/you/we/they won't.
	he/she/it/

Question words

What will you do? Where will you go?

Expressions of future time

tomorrow   tomorrow morning   tomorrow afternoon   next week   next month   next year   in two days   in three months   in five years

Use

You use the future simple:

- to make a prediction or express an opinion about the future. (See Lesson 12.)
  I think most people will need English for their jobs.

- to talk about decisions you make at the moment of speaking. (See Lesson 13.)
  I'll give you the money right now.

- to talk about things you are not sure will happen with *probably* and *perhaps*. (See Lesson 13.)
  He'll probably spend three weeks there. Perhaps he'll stay two days in Rio.

- to offer to do something. (See Lesson 13.)
  OK, I'll buy some food.

Verb patterns

There are several possible patterns after certain verbs which involve -*ing* form verbs and infinitive constructions with or without *to*.

-*ing* form verbs

You can put an -*ing* form verb after certain verbs. (See Lesson 4.)
I love walking. She likes swimming. They hate lying on the beach.

Remember that *would like to do something* refers to an activity at a specific time in the future.
I'd like to go to the movies next Saturday.

Try not to confuse it with *like doing something* which refers to an activity you enjoy all the time.
I like going to the movies. I go most weekends.

To + infinitive

You can put *to* + infinitive after many verbs. Here are some of them:

agree   decide   go   have   hope   earn   leave like   need   offer   start   try   want

Use

You use *to* + infinitive with *(be) going to* and *would like to*. (See below.)

Have to

You use *have to* and *have got to* to talk about something you're obliged or strongly advised to do:
You have to wear a helmet.

In negatives, you use *don't have to*:
You don't have to go to work on Sunday.
Don't have to means that something is not necessary.

Going to

You use *(be) going to*:
- to talk about future intentions or plans. (See Lesson 11.)
  I'm going to be a doctor. (I'm studying medicine.)
- to talk about things which are arranged and sure to happen with *(be) going to*. (See Lesson 13.)
  I'm going to visit South America. I've bought my ticket.

You often use the present continuous and not *going to* with *come* and *go*.
Are you coming tonight?
NOT ~~Are you going to come tonight?~~
He's going to South America.
NOT ~~He's going to go to South America.~~

Would like to

You use *would like to*:

● to talk about ambitions, hopes, or preferences.
  (See Lesson 11.)
  I'd like to speak English fluently.

Have (got)

Form

You use the contracted form in spoken and informal written English.

Affirmative		Negative	
I		I	
you	've (have) got	you	haven't (have not) got
we		we	
they		they	
he		he	
she	's (has) got	she	hasn't (has not) got
it		it	

Questions	Short answers
Have I/you/we/they got?	Yes, I/you/we/they have.
	No, I/you/we/they haven't.
Has he/she/it got?	Yes, he/she/it has.
	No, he/she/it hasn't.

Use

You use *have (got)* to talk about facilities, possession, or relationship. (See Lesson 10.)
I've got a new car. or *I have a new car.*

You don't use *have got* to talk about a habit or routine.
I often have lunch out. NOT *I often have got lunch out.*

You don't usually use *have got* in the past. You use the past simple of *have.*
I had a headache yesterday. NOT *I had got a headache.*

Questions

You can form questions in two ways:

● with a question word such as *who, what, which, where, how, why.*
  What's your name?

● without a question word.
  Are you American?

You can put a noun after *what* and *which.* (See Lesson 1.)
What time is it? Which road will you take?

You often say *what* to give the idea that there is more choice.
What books have you read lately?

You can put an adjective or an adverb after *how.*
(See Lessons 15 and 20.)
How much is it? How long does it take by car? How fast can you drive?

You can use *who, what,* or *which* as pronouns to ask about the subject of the sentence. You don't use *do* or *did.*
(See Lessons 1 and 7.)
What's your first name?
Who invented the first traveler's check?

You can use *who, what,* or *which* and other question words to ask about the object of the sentence. You use *do* or *did.*
(See Lessons 1 and 7.)
What did he call his invention?

Articles

You can find the main uses of articles in Lesson 3. Here are some extra details.

You use *an* for nouns which begin with a vowel.
an armchair

You use *one* if you want to emphasise the number.
One hundred and twenty-two.

Before vowels you pronounce *the* /ði:/.

You do not use the definite article with parts of the body.
You use a possessive adjective.
I'm washing my hair.

Plurals

You can find the main rules for forming plurals in Lesson 3.

Possessives

You can find the main uses of the possessive *'s* in Lesson 9.
You can find a list of possessive adjectives in Lesson 9.

Expressions of quantity

Countable and uncountable nouns

Countable nouns have both a singular and a plural form.
(See Lesson 15.)
an apple – some apples, a melon – some melons,
a potato – some potatoes, a cup – (not) many cups,
a cookie – a few cookies

Uncountable nouns do not usually have a plural form.
some wine, some cheese, some fruit, (not) much meat, a little coffee

If you talk about different kinds of uncountable nouns they become countable.
Beaujolais and Bordeaux are both French wines.

Expressions with countable or uncountable nouns

You can put countable or uncountable nouns with these expressions of quantity.
lots of apples, lots of cheese, hardly any apples, hardly any cheese, a lot of fruit, a lot of potatoes.

Some and any

(See Lesson 15.)

Affirmative   *There's some milk in the refrigerator.*
               There are some apples on the table.

Negative   *I haven't got any brothers.*
               There isn't any cheese.

Questions

You usually use *any* for questions.
Is there any sugar?

You can use *some* in questions when you are making an offer or a request, and you expect the answer to be *yes*.
Would you like some coffee?
Can I have some sugar, please?

Much and many

You use *many* with countable nouns and *much* with uncountable nouns. (See Lesson 15.)
How many eggs would you like?
How much butter do you need?

Too much/many, not enough, fewer, less, and more

You can put a countable noun in the plural after *too many*, *not enough*, and *fewer*.
There are too many people.
There aren't enough clean rivers.
In the United States there are fewer men than women.

You can put an uncountable noun after *too much*, *not enough*, *more*, and *less*.
There's too much noise. There isn't enough farmland.
There's more pollution.

You can put an adjective after *too* or between *not* and *enough*.
The sea is too polluted. The air isn't clean enough.

Making comparisons

Comparative and superlative adjectives

Form

You add -*er* to most adjectives for the comparative form, and -*est* for the superlative form. (See Lesson 18.)
cold colder coldest   *cheap cheaper cheapest*

You add -*r* to adjectives ending in -*e* for the comparative form and -*st* for the superlative form.
large larger largest   *fine finer finest*

You add -*ier* to adjectives ending in -*y* for the comparative form, and -*iest* for the superlative form.

happy happier happiest
friendly friendlier friendliest

You double the last letter of adjectives ending in -*g*, -*t*, or -*n*.
hot hotter hottest
thin thinner thinnest

You use *more* for the comparative form and *most* for the superlative form of longer adjectives.
expensive more expensive most expensive
important more important most important

Some adjectives have irregular comparative and superlative forms.
good better best bad worse worst

More than, less than, as … as

- You put *than* before the object of comparison. (See Lesson 19.)
  Children wear more casual clothes than their parents.
- You use *less … than* to change the focus of the comparison.
  Parents wear less casual clothes than their children.
- You can put *much* before the comparative adjective, *more*, or *less* to emphasize it.
  They're much less formal than they were.
- You use *as … as* to show something is the same.
  They're as casual as teenagers all over the world.
- You use not *as … as* to show something is different.
  Dresses are not as popular as in Western countries.

So, because

- You can join two sentences with *so* to describe a consequence.
  She often took the plane so she didn't look at the safety instructions.
- You can join the same two sentences with *because* to describe a reason.
  She didn't look at the safety instructions because she often took the plane.

Prepositions of place

(See Lesson 14.)

Prepositions of time and place: *in, at, on, to*

(See Lesson 16.)

Use

You use *in*:

- with times of the day: *in the morning, in the afternoon.*
- with months of the year: *in March, in September*
- with years: *in 1996, in 1872*
- with places: *in New York, in Mexico City, in the bank*

You use *at*:
- with times of the day: *at night, at seven o'clock*
- with places: *at the theater, at the stadium*

You use *on*:
- with days, dates: *on Friday, on July 15th*

You use *to*:
- with places: *Let's go to Seattle.*

Adverbs of frequency

Use

You use an adverb of frequency to say how often things happen. (See Lesson 1.)

They always take their shoes off.
We usually take wine or flowers.
We often wear jeans and sweaters.
We sometimes arrive about fifteen minutes after.
We never ask personal questions.

Tapescripts

Lesson 1 **Speaking and Listening, activity 2**

Situation 1

PAT Yumio! Great to see you. You look great!
YUMIO How are you, Pat?
PAT We're all fine. Come in, come in.
YUMIO Pat, this is my friend Rosario Rodriguez.
PAT Hello, Rosario, how do you do? I'm very pleased to meet you.
ROSARIO How do you do?
PAT Come in. We're in the back room, come on through. Now, when was the last time we got together?

Situation 2

WOMAN Excuse me!
WAITER Yes, can I help you?
WOMAN Yes, I'd like a Coke, please.
WAITER Sure. Small, medium, or large?
WOMAN Sorry, I don't understand.
WAITER What size? Would you like a big, small, or a medium Coke?
WOMAN Oh, small, please.
WAITER Here you go.
WOMAN Thank you. How much is it?
WAITER Ninety cents.

Lesson 1 **Speaking and Listening, activity 3**

1. What's your first name?
2. Where do you live?
3. Are you married?
4. What do you do?
5. Do you have any brothers and sisters?
6. Where do you come from?

Lesson 2 **Listening, activity 1**

Speaker 1

JO-ANN I get up around seven o'clock and have breakfast. Then I have to leave home at about eight, I guess. It takes me about forty minutes to ride the bus downtown and start work at about nine.
Q Do you like your job?
JO-ANN It's OK. Some days it's fine, some days you get some real tricky customers.
Q Do you get time off for lunch?
JO-ANN Sure, I stop around twelve-thirty and then at one o'clock I take a walk in the park—just to get some fresh air, you know. If the weather's OK, I'll have a sandwich or something there.
Q Mmm. Does it get busy in the afternoon?
JO-ANN No more than in the morning, I guess. When the bank's open, people call at all times.
Q So when do you leave work?
JO-ANN I leave work at about five in the evening, and sometimes I take the bus back home. Other times I go to a bar or a coffee shop with my friends. I guess I usually go to bed around eleven-thirty.

Speaker 2

GEORGE I get up very early these days, much earlier than when I was at work, at about six o'clock, I guess.
Q Why so early?
GEORGE Oh, I like to see the sun rise, have a walk on the beach, you know. If it's hot, I go for a swim in the sea before breakfast.
Q And what time do you have breakfast?
GEORGE I get breakfast ready for about eight-fifteen and take it up to Hilary who's still in bed. Then we go shopping in the local mall, meet some friends, have lunch, that sort of thing.
Q What time do you have lunch, then?
GEORGE At about half-past twelve, I guess. And in the afternoon, I go for another walk, maybe play a little golf, have a swim, go down to the community center to join Hilary.
Q And what about in the evening?
GEORGE Well, I meet my friends at about five-thirty and have a drink or two at the golf club. We talk for about an hour or so, then I go home for dinner at seven o'clock. Maybe we have friends around, maybe we go for dinner, it just depends. But most nights we're in bed by ten-thirty. It's a great life!

Lesson 5 **Listening and Vocabulary, activity 2**

Conversation 1

WOMAN Good morning.
TELLER Good morning. How may I help you?
WOMAN I'd like three hundred dollars worth of Italian lira, please.
TELLER Traveler's checks or cash?
WOMAN Traveler's checks.
TELLER Could I have your passport, please? Thank you. Would you sign and date them, please?
WOMAN Here you are.
TELLER That makes four hundred and twenty-one thousand lira.
WOMAN Thank you.
TELLER Thank you. Have a nice trip.

Conversation 2

WAITRESS Good evening, sir. A table for two?
MAN Yes, but could we sit by the window, please?
WAITRESS Certainly sir. Come this way. Here you are sir, ma'am. Can I take your coats?
WOMAN Thank you.
WAITRESS My name is Lori, and I'll be your server tonight. Can I get you a drink while you look at the menu?
MAN Not for me, thank you.
WOMAN No, thanks. I think we'll just have some wine with the meal, please
WAITRESS I recommend the lamb this evening. It's cooked with spices, it's a Lebanese dish, specialty of the chef. I'm sure you'll like it. It comes with mixed vegetables.
MAN Sounds great!
WOMAN Well, I'd like to have a look at the menu anyway.
WAITRESS Certainly, ma'am. I'll come back when you're ready to order.

Conversation 3

WOMAN Hi. I need a round trip ticket to San Diego, leaving tomorrow.

TRAVEL AGENT Will you be spending the weekend in San Diego?

WOMAN Yes. I'm coming back on Tuesday—the 12th.

TRAVEL AGENT OK. Uh, that's going to be $279 plus tax. Are you a "Miles Plus" member?

WOMAN I don't think so. What is it?

TRAVEL AGENT Well, the airline keeps track of all the miles you fly with them, and when you reach 25,000 miles, you get a free round trip ticket to any destination in the U.S.

WOMAN Sounds great! Sign me up!

Conversation 4

MAN What would you recommend for a cough?

PHARMACIST Well, I can give you some cough medicine, but if it's very bad, you ought to see a doctor.

MAN No, it's not too bad. I thought I'd try something over the counter first.

PHARMACIST Have you got a headache and a fever?

MAN Yes.

PHARMACIST Well, try this medicine for your cough and these tablets for the headache and fever. They're a kind of aspirin which you dissolve in hot water.

MAN Thank you. How much is that?

PHARMACIST That'll be eight dollars and fifty cents, please.

MAN Thank you.

Fluency 1 **Listening and Reading, activity 3**

KELLY Hello, Joe. How are you?

JOE Hi, Kelly. Fine, thanks. Hey, you look great today! That's a beautiful dress.

KELLY Thanks. How was your weekend?

JOE OK.

TEACHER Good morning, everyone. Uh, my name is Steve Smith. You can call me Steve. How are you all today?

JOE Hi, Steve! We're all fine.

KELLY Good morning, Mr. Smith.

TEACHER Please sit down, everyone.

DAVE Oh, I'm sorry I'm late.

TEACHER No problem, we've just started. Now, take out your textbooks and turn to page 15.

JOE Can I ask a question? Can you tell me what *Buenos dias* means?

TEACHER It means *good day* or *hello* in Spanish. OK, I'd like you to work in pairs.

DAVE Is it OK if I work with you, Kelly?

KELLY Yes, of course.

Fluency 1 **Functions, activity 4**

A B C D E F G H I J K L M N O P Q R S T U V W X Y Z

Fluency 1 **Functions, activity 5**

A H J K
B C D E G P T V Z
F L M N S X
I Y
O
Q U W
R

Fluency 1 **Reading and Listening, activity 2**

Q OK, Jennifer. Now you're taking a Spanish course, aren't you?

JENNIFER Yeah, I am.

Q Is it all right if I ask you a few questions about what you do in the classroom, classroom behavior, that kind of thing?

JENNIFER Sure.

Q OK, my first question is: Do you greet people when you come into class and if so, what do you say?

JENNIFER You mean do I greet my fellow students or do I greet the teacher?

Q Well, I guess both.

JENNIFER Well, yeah, I greet my fellow students. I probably say "Hi, how are you doing?" and like if I know their names, "Hi, Bill, what's up?" or something like that. To the teacher I guess I usually say "Good evening."

Q And do you stand up when your teacher comes into class?

JENNIFER Stand up? No, we don't usually do that.

Q What do you call your teacher?

JENNIFER Uh well, at the beginning of the year when we didn't know her so well we called her Ms. Sanchez. But now we usually call her Maria.

Q I see. So now you know her better you use her first name.

JENNIFER Yeah. We call her Maria.

Q Right. And if you're late for class, do you say anything? Do you say you're sorry you're late?

JENNIFER Uh, yes, of course. I mean I would always apologise for being late. I'd say something like "I'm sorry I'm late."

Q OK. Next question. Who do you think should talk most in a language class, the teacher or the students?

JENNIFER Oh boy, that's a hard one. Well, I guess ideally the students should talk most because that means they're practicing the language. But I think at the beginning of our course Maria, the teacher, talked most. But I guess now that we've gotten a bit better at Spanish, it's really the students who talk most. It's a great class, we're all really enthusiastic and we want to learn, so we talk.

Q Well, that's great. But do you only speak when you're spoken to?

JENNIFER No, no, I mean if we're asked a question, yeah, we speak, but you know a lot of times we ask questions and we might have an idea, you know, something to say on a subject and then, well, no, we wouldn't wait to be spoken to, I mean to be asked, we would go right ahead and say what we wanted to say.

Q Are you expected to work with other students?

JENNIFER Work with other students? How do you mean?

Q Well, I guess, work in pairs, do an exercise together.

JENNIFER Oh, yeah, I mean we do a lot of our practice in pairs and in groups. And when we're doing an exercise we help each other.

Q So do you think it's OK to cheat sometimes?

JENNIFER Cheat? Uh uh. I mean, that depends what you mean. I don't think it's OK to cheat in a test, you know, I mean, when you're supposed to be working on your own and your score on the test is being used to assess your progress. No. But exercises in class, I mean homework perhaps, I mean then I think it's OK to help each other—I don't know if that counts as cheating!

Q Oh, OK. Now in class, you've already said that you ask questions.

JENNIFER Yeah, of course.

Q Right, but do you ask them during the class or do you wait until the end?

JENNIFER Oh, definitely usually during the class.

Q And in your language lessons, which of these things would you expect? I've got a list here—can you take a look at this list?

JENNIFER Sure. All right, let me see... quizzes, um yeah sometimes; exams, yeah maybe at the end of the course. Dictionaries, oh, definitely, we use them a lot. Other reference books? No, not usually. Exercises, songs and role plays: yeah, we do a lot of those. Yeah, I mean in fact looking at this list, I would say we have all of these things, except perhaps field trips.

Q Which of these things do you expect in lessons on other subjects?

JENNIFER Um, well, that's kind of hard to say as I don't take any other classes. Sorry, I can't help you there!

Q Never mind. OK, tell me how do you know when a class is over?

JENNIFER Well, there's no bell or anything like that to say that time's up. Uh, I guess the teacher usually tells us. She'll say something like, you know, "OK, that's it for this week, now for homework can you do this or that", you know, something like that.

Q And do you wait for the teacher to leave before you leave?

JENNIFER Oh, no, we don't do that. I mean, some students leave straight away and some wait behind to talk to each other or, you know, to the teacher. It's not a very formal class.

Q It sounds like fun. OK, Jennifer, thanks for your help.

JENNIFER You're welcome.

Lesson 8   **Listening and Speaking, activity 2**

I arrived in this town quite late, about ten o'clock, I guess, and looked for somewhere to stay. I didn't have a reservation anywhere, because I didn't expect to stay there. The main hotel was full, but the concierge told me there was a small motel down the road. I left the car where it was and I went down the road and actually I walked right past the motel, because I saw there were no lights on. I knocked on the door—there was no bell, or anything—and a man opened the door. He was unshaven and wearing a very dirty T-shirt, and the television was on. I asked if he had a room and without saying a word, he picked up a key from behind the desk and pushed a registration card at me. I wrote my name, but not my address, I don't know why, I felt there was something wrong. I saw that all the keys were on their hooks, so either all the other guests were out or I was the only person staying there. I followed him along a dimly-lit passage—most of the light bulbs had burned out—and he showed me a very dusty room. He gave me the key and closed the door. I sat down on the tiny single bed and wondered what to do. It was a horrible room with a sink, but no shower or toilet or anything. I decided I wanted to check out right away but I was frightened by the man in the office. I ran out of my room and walked quickly past his office, but he didn't look up. I quickly said, "I've left my suitcase in my car", and ran off, up the street, and locked myself in the car—I was so scared. I slept in the car that night!

Lesson 9   **Vocabulary and Listening, activity 2**

I've got a big family, actually. My grandmother lives with my mother and father, and her name is Pat. Then I have a brother whose name is Ray, who lives in Rochester, and a sister, Kelly, who lives in Syracuse. My aunt's name is Christine and my uncle's name is Tony. Then, of course, there's my husband Larry. His family comes from Buffalo, and that's where we live now. Oh, I nearly forgot, my mother's name is Carol and my father's, Craig. We're very close.

Lesson 10   **Vocabulary and Listening, activity 2**

Q What's it like living in Taipei?
LAURA Oh, I love it! The people are so friendly and helpful, and it's big, but not too big, you know?
Q What's the population?
LAURA About three and a half million, I think... I'm not sure. But it doesn't feel really congested, like a lot of other big cities. It's fairly polluted, I guess... nothing like L.A., though! And it's got everything... parks, museums... fantastic museums!... restaurants to die for...
Q Is it very industrialized?
LAURA Oh, sure... out in the suburbs there are, you know, the factories and the industrial estates, and... uh... the city center is pretty modern. But there is still a lot of the "old" Taipei... like Wanhua, which has houses and shops and temples and family shrines that are all about 100 years old. I go down there a lot to take photos and just watch people.
Q What are the people like?
LAURA Oh, really friendly and helpful... I'm taking Chinese classes at the university now, but when I first arrived I was totally lost, and people kept helping me out... taking me places, and translating for me...
Q Wow! Uh... is Taipei expensive?
LAURA Well, it's getting that way, but I guess I get paid pretty well, so it doesn't seem... I mean, clothes and food are really cheap. But I pay about twice as much rent as I would in the U.S., and my apartment is, well, tiny!

Lesson 10   **Vocabulary and Listening, activity 5**

SPEAKER 1 It's quite cheap to live here, although in certain parts of town houses are really very expensive. Everyday things in the stores are very cheap compared with the U.S., although clothes can cost a lot.
SPEAKER 2 Oh, it's incredible, I mean, there are so many cars and trucks. You see, the railroad system is not very extensive so everything has to go by road. But at rush hour in the center of town, it's so busy.
SPEAKER 3 It's a very interesting place to visit, although I wouldn't call the buildings beautiful. But the palace is quite fascinating and well worth spending a day on. And then there are some wonderful churches and mosques.
SPEAKER 4 It's really small, about one hundred thousand people, and the city center is really very compact, although the suburbs stretch for about five miles in each direction.
SPEAKER 5 It rains all the time, it's famous for that. Even in the middle of the summer you are never certain that the sun will shine all day, so it's difficult to make plans for any outdoor activities.
SPEAKER 6 Well, you can still walk the streets at night and not feel nervous that someone's going to attack you. But I think it's a good idea to be sensible and keep your money and valuables safe in your jacket. You never know, it can happen anywhere, can't it?

Fluency 2   **Listening and Speaking, activity 2**

1.
JERRY What are you doing this evening?
KATE Not much.
JERRY Would you like to go to a movie?
KATE Sure. What's on?
JERRY There's a new Quentin Tarantino movie that just came out...
KATE Great! What time does it start?
JERRY Seven o'clock. Why don't we leave here at a quarter after six?
KATE Make it six o'clock. The traffic is pretty bad at that time.
JERRY Six o'clock, then. See you downstairs.
KATE OK. See you later .

2.
LENNY What time does the plane leave?
DIANA Ten thirty.
LENNY And what time is it now?
DIANA It's about nine fifteen.
LENNY How long does it take to get to the airport?
DIANA About half an hour.
LENNY Well, we ought to leave right away, I guess. I don't want to miss it.
DIANA Relax! We've got plenty of time.

Fluency 2   **Listening and Speaking, activity 6**

BILL OK. I've been asked to talk a little about daily routines in the U.S. and the times people do things. First I'd have to say that this is a huge country and it's very difficult to say what is typical. I mean, everybody's different. But I'll give it a try.

Getting up in the morning. Well this kind of depends on your job. I mean, yeah, I guess a lot of people do get up at about 7 o'clock. Probably most people, yeah.

As for starting work, well, again that depends on what you do, but, yes, working hours in the U.S. are generally considered to be nine to five, so I guess it's OK to say that people generally start work at nine o'clock.

There's usually a coffee break at eleven o'clock. Um. No, I'd have to say that's wrong. People drink coffee all the time. I don't think there's a specific time, a specific break when they drink coffee. No.

You have to be on time for appointments. Yeah, you do. Business appointments that is. You're expected to be on time for business appointments. It's kind of different for friends, though. As long as you're not too late. I think it's OK to be late for a meeting with a friend: maybe ten to fifteen minutes or so.

Lunch can be anytime from noon. I wouldn't say that everyone eats lunch exactly at noon. No, I'd say that's wrong. I mean, in a lot of companies lunch is from 1 to 2, so, no, I don't think it's true to say that lunch is *usually* at noon. Though it often is.

In the U.S. it's not common to spend time with co-workers after work. We usually like to get back home to our families after work.

Dinner *can* be at eight o'clock but again, I don't think you can say it's *usually* at eight. Like lunch, different people eat at different times. I'd say that if you're invited to friends for dinner that *is* usually at eight, but with your family, well, you might eat a lot earlier than that, especially if you've got young kids.

Most people *are* in bed before midnight. I guess that's probably true, but there are a lot of people who like to party all night! They aren't *most* people though. I guess if you're talking about *most* people, then, yeah, in bed before midnight is about right.

Fluency 2 Functions, activity 3

1.
A OK. Here's your boarding pass. Boarding time will be ten thirty from gate 38.
B Thank you.

2.
MOTHER Come on, John. Finish your cereal quickly or you'll miss the bus. Come on, it's ten after eight.
JOHN Oh, Mom, do I have to go to school today?
MOTHER Yes, you do!

3.
This is Cooper and Ramirez. We are sorry that there's no one here to take your call. The office will be open again tomorrow at eight thirty A.M. If you would like to leave a message, please speak after the tone.

4.
A Excuse me, can you tell me what track the nine-fifteen to Boston leaves from?
B Track 10, sir.

Lesson 12 Listening, activity 2

Q Maggie, um... I'd like to ask you first, um... at what age do people start learning English these days?
MAGGIE Um... well, in many countries children start learning English when they go to school, but I think in some countries they're starting to teach English to much younger children and I think this will become more and more common around the world.
GREG Yeah, that's right 'cause I know that um... in some countries they're even having English lessons for six-year-old children so, they'll certainly be learning as soon as they start school, if not before.
Q I see. And do you think, um... English will soon be the universal language?
MAGGIE Oh, I think most adults already speak some English, um... even if it's only a word or two here and there, because, well, English is very common and very useful.
GREG Mmm... I...
Q What about you, Greg?
GREG Well, I think Maggie's absolutely right. Because, if you think about it, already there are so many words, for example to do with computers, um, you know, that are in English and that are used internationally, for example, um... "radio, television, hamburger," these are all international words—English words though. So I think pretty soon there'll be very few people who don't speak English, not just a few words but, you know, really communicating in it.
Q And do you think, Maggie, that teachers will start using English to teach other subjects, you know, for instance, geography or science, and that it'll be used in schools all over the world?
MAGGIE Yes, I sure do. I think that teachers will start experimenting with that. I think in many ways it's the best way to learn English.
GREG Mmm...
Q Greg?
GREG Um... I'm not so sure. I think some classes will be in English for

sure, um... for example, science. But I think most others won't be in English. There's no reason why every single subject should be taught in English.
Q Right. Now, what about North American life, culture, and institutions, do you think that it's important to know about those?
MAGGIE No, not at all. I mean, I don't think that English as a language has anything to do with, like, mom's apple pie and the American Dream. I mean, it's an international language and, um... it can be used for communication between people who don't know each other's language, um... as a tool really. So, I don't think that the cultural roots of English are important at all.
GREG Well, I disagree, because I think you have to understand, er... the culture of a country, just because there are some words that mean different things to different people depending on what country they're in, for example... the word "family" ... it means one thing to North Americans and another to South Americans. Uh... the word "police" means different things to different people. You always have to know something about the background and the culture of a country before you can fully understand the language.
Q Mmm. What about in the workplace? How important is English there, what's its role?
MAGGIE Well, I think it's really important and I think more and more people will use it at work—it's, it's... easily understood wherever you come from and I think, well, actually, everyone will need to use more English for their work.
Q Greg?
GREG Um... I think some people will need to use more English, particularly people working in big companies who have to travel a lot and do a lot of business between different countries, but I think for the majority of the population in any country, uh, you know, who don't... who aren't involved in international business or moving around or traveling, then I think they'll continue to do business in their own language.
Q And the traditional language class as we know it—do you think that that will continue or will there be other forms of teaching, such as, you know, teaching involving television and computers, and so forth?
MAGGIE Well, I think that the traditional language class will still exist. Um... I think that personal contact is very important with the language teacher and, um... of course, there is more than one person in a class, you can interact with the other students and I think that that's much more valuable than just staring at a computer screen or, you know, listening to cassettes.
Q Mmm. Do you agree with that, Greg?
GREG Not entirely. We live in a computer age now, and I think that computers and other ... videos for example—all those interactive programs that you use with videos—will allow people to learn foreign languages in a different way on their own, so that you don't have to depend on teachers and other students. I'm not sure, but I think that's how it'll be.
Q And finally, Maggie, do you think that English will ever become more important than the language of the native speaker?
MAGGIE Well, no. I think obviously English is important, but I think your own language and your own culture and traditions are more important to you and I think it's good to respect those and to hold on to them.
GREG Yes, I agree. I think it would be very arrogant to think that English would be more important than your own language, I mean, 'cause your language is part of your culture and your personal identity and your national identity, isn't it?
MAGGIE Mmm. I think so.
Q Thank you very much.
GREG No problem!

Lesson 13 **Listening, activity 2**

CATHY So, what are you going to do this summer?
RYAN I'm going to South America.
CATHY Great!
RYAN I'm going to be traveling around a lot and I'll probably spend three weeks there.
CATHY So, where are you going?
RYAN To start out, I'm going to fly to Rio and maybe I'll stay there for a couple of days.
CATHY Do you know anyone there?
RYAN No, but I've always wanted to go to Rio. It's supposed to be totally awesome. And I'll probably go up the Sugar Loaf mountain, in the cable car, like all the tourists.
CATHY And where are you going after that?
RYAN I'm going to fly to Santiago in Chile, where I've got some friends. We'll probably spend some time doing some sightseeing and then we're going to lie on the beach for a few days in Valparaiso, which is on the coast, not far away from Santiago. Then I'm flying to Lima where I'm going to meet my girlfriend and then we're going to visit Machu Picchu in the mountains.
CATHY And visit the ruins? Oh, fantastic!
RYAN Yeah, it should be pretty cool. And then we'll probably go somewhere on the Amazon. I don't know where yet, but I'd like to spend a week in the jungle. Then we'll probably fly home.
CATHY Well, have a great time!

Lesson 13 **Listening, Activity 4**

CATHY Do you have a good guide book?
RYAN No, I don't. But I'm going to get one. It's on my list of things to buy before I go.
CATHY Well, they say the best one is "South American Handbook."
RYAN Really? Well, I'll get it when I go downtown.
CATHY Look, I'm going downtown right now because I need to do some shopping. I'll buy it for you at the bookstore, if you want.
RYAN Really?
CATHY Yeah, sure.
RYAN Well, I'll give you the money for it right now.
CATHY OK, and I'll bring it to your place tonight. Who knows, maybe I'll borrow it from you someday.
RYAN OK. Thanks a lot.

Lesson 15 **Grammar, activity 2**

A We need some water. How many bottles do we need?
B Two. And we don't have any fruit. Do you want to get some peaches?
A OK. Do we have any coffee?
B No, how much do we need?
A Just one pound.

Lesson 15 **Listening and Speaking, activity 2**

Q So, Pat, you've lived in the United States for five years. Where do you live?
PAT In San Francisco.
Q Uh-huh. And, um… we were wondering what typical meals were like for you. I mean, what do you have for a typical breakfast?
PAT Well, a lot of people eat a lot—you know, steak, eggs, hash browns, and so forth… but I can't eat that much. I have coffee, and I like cereal, so, I'll eat grape nuts or granola, something like that. But, usually I just have, um… fruit and… juicing is very big now, of course.
Q Uh huh.
PAT I'll juice a lot of fruit in a blender.
Q Is there any fruit that's especially good?
PAT Um… apricots are very good. Apricots, oranges, bananas.
Q And, when you juice things, you make a mixture of these fruits, do you?
PAT Yes, I basically just throw everything in, and, um, juice it and then drink and then that keeps me going for most of the morning.
Q Hmm. How about lunch? Do you have lunch?

PAT Well, if I'm going to eat lunch, I tend to go more for, um… either light pasta dishes, or vegetable platter where you have, you know, beans, courgettes, aubergines, that sort of thing.
Q Courgettes?
PAT Oh, I mean zucchini!
Q And aubergines are…?
PAT That's eggplant.
Q Aubergine, right!
PAT Old habits die hard! But, um… more often than not, probably just a sub sandwich. Full of meat…
Q And is that your main meal?
PAT No, no, no. The main meal is in the evening.
Q And what do you have then?
PAT Um… well, San Francisco is… you can eat very well, um… if you go to seafood restaurants, and so… I like a lot of seafood, so, um… my favorite is soft shell crabs…
Q Delicious!
PAT … with steamed vegetables. Maybe I'll have some sort of seafood chowder before that, and a mixed salad, and finish it all with key-lime pie, perhaps.
Q Mmm!

Q Karen, how long have you been living in Hong Kong?
KAREN Just over a year now.
Q And have you gotten used to the way of life there?
KAREN Yes, I think so. It's a very upbeat place, so you have to adapt.
Q Yes, what sort of things do you eat? What's a typical breakfast for you?
KAREN Um… well, during the week I'm very busy. I have to get to the school where I work quite early, so I have just a quick breakfast—but a substantial one. Um… so usually cereal, toast, orange juice, a cup of coffee.
Q Very healthy!
KAREN Uh-huh.
Q Right. And then, er… do you have lunch?
KAREN If I have time, yes. I run out and grab a sandwich, or a baked potato from a local fast-food place, if I can.
Q So, no Chinese delicacies?
KAREN Not at lunch time, no. No time!
Q Yeah, that's not your main meal, then? The main meal is dinner?
KAREN In the evening.
Q Yes, yes. And then, what do you eat?
KAREN Well, um… we get together—several teachers—and we go out to a Chinese restaurant, or um… there is food from all over the world in Hong Kong… Japanese, Indonesian—and we eat there. Um… a favorite Chinese meal is "dim sum."
Q Uh-huh. What's that?
KAREN Well, it's like a dumpling, um… which they steam, and inside are different types of meat or vegetables. They're fantastic.
Q Yes. And, are there any, um… desserts, any sweet things to eat?
KAREN Chinese desserts are very sticky, and a bit too sweet for me, so I usually avoid them.
Q Yeah. Thank you.

Fluency 3 **Speaking and Listening, activity 2**

CLERK Hi there. What can I do for you?
MAN I'd like a pack of Marlboro, please.
CLERK Soft pack or box?
MAN Box, please.
CLERK There you are, one pack of Marlboro. That's two-fifty. Will that be all for you today, sir?
MAN Oh, I need a gallon of milk.
CLERK Right over there in the refrigerator, sir. Help yourself.
MAN Right. And do you have today's paper?
CLERK We sure do. That's fifty cents...and three twenty-nine for the milk, two fifty for the Marlboro...That's six twenty-nine altogether, sir.
MAN Here you are.
CLERK Out of ten? That's thirty, forty, fifty, seven dollars, eight, nine, and ten.
MAN Thanks.
CLERK Thank *you* sir. Have a nice day.

Fluency 3 **Functions, activity 1**

Five hundred and five.
Four hundred and seventy-eight
Three thousand, five hundred and sixty-three.
Forty-five thousand, seven hundred and eighty-one

Fluency 3 **Functions, activity 3**

$10.50
12,314
204
$19.99
138,526
$20.50

Fluency 3 **Speaking and Listening 2, activity 2**

Q OK, Mei and Jorge. I'd like to talk to you about prices of things in your country.
JORGE OK.
MEI OK.
Q First a gallon of milk. How much would a gallon of milk cost in Brazil, Jorge?
JORGE Oh, I guess about $3.
Q And in Malaysia, Mei?
MEI I think about $3.
Q Right. What about a pound of fish?
JORGE I don't know. Perhaps around $1.30.
MEI I think in Malaysia a pound of fish would be about $2.60.
Q OK. How about a meal in a restaurant, Mei?
MEI Well, that depends on the restaurant. I mean there are expensive restaurants and there are cheap restaurants.
Q What about say an average meal for two?
MEI Probably around $20.
JORGE I think in Brazil an average meal for two would cost about $20 to $25.
Q And a bottle of wine?
JORGE Anything from $5 upwards in a supermarket to $10 upwards in a restaurant, depending on how good the wine was.
MEI I guess about $15.
Q Good. Now suppose you want to go to the movies. How much is a ticket for the movies going to cost you?
JORGE Oh, that I know. I go to the movies a lot. In Brazil that would cost you $7.
MEI For us that would be $3.
Q I see. OK. Now you are going to buy a new car. You know, just an ordinary family car. But new, not second-hand. How much?
MEI Probably about $20,000 to $60,000.
JORGE I think in my country it would be anything around $12,000 upwards.
Q Right. Something cheaper now. A newspaper.

MEI That would cost you 50 cents
JORGE In Brazil probably $1.
Q How about ... a new television?
JORGE A new television? Well, I think you could probably buy one for around $350.
Q What about in Malaysia, Mei?
MEI I'm not sure. Maybe for a new television you would have to pay around $200 to $300.
Q OK. Now how about a house? Again I think we're talking about, you know, an average family house, not a huge mansion or anything. Jorge?
JORGE I've never bought a house, but I guess you'd have to pay, well, about $200,000.
Q How about you, Mei?
MEI No, I've never bought a house either. I think in Malaysia people pay around $120,000.
Q I see. Quite a difference there! OK, back to cheaper things. How much is a gallon of gas in Brazil, Jorge?
JORGE Gas for the car? Um, I think now it's around $2.26 a gallon.
Q What about a gallon of gas in Malaysia, Mei? How much?
MEI I think around $1.68.
Q Well, that's been very interesting. Thank you both very much.
MEI You're welcome.
JORGE No problem.

Lesson 16 **Listening and Speaking, activity 1**

Q So, Ken, tell me. What is karaoke?
KEN Well, basically, it's singing along to some recorded music. You have a microphone and there's some music playing and you can sing the words—in tune, if you can.
Q Where do you do this?
KEN Well, all over Tokyo there are karaoke bars where you can go with friends, have a drink and sing karaoke. It's very popular.
Q Who does it?
KEN Anyone. Anyone who feels brave enough to sing in public, it could be you or me or anyone.
Q After a couple of beers, maybe! What kind of music do you sing?
KEN Well, it's traditional Japanese music for older people, but for young people it's mostly well-known Western pop songs, you know, Frank Sinatra, Phil Collins, Madonna, that sort of thing.
Q Why do people enjoy it?
KEN I don't know, really. It's a chance to show that you could be a pop singer too, I guess. It's also a way of showing how close you are to your friends. If you can make a fool of yourself in front of these people, then you really are good friends, you know?
Q What about tango, Marybeth?
MARYBETH Tango is a very exotic kind of dance in Latin America, and it's especially popular in Argentina, where it originally came from.
Q And where is it performed?
MARYBETH In concert halls or theaters, or maybe small bars.
Q And who performs the tango?
MARYBETH Well, in the theater they're mostly professional dancers, although in dance halls and bars, everyone tries to dance the tango if the music is right.
Q And what is the music they use?
MARYBETH Well, tango is both the dance and the music. You dance the tango to music specially written for it. They use the violin and the accordion quite a lot for it.
Q And why do you think people enjoy it?
MARYBETH Well, it's a very passionate dance. It's full of life, it's great fun.
Q Can you dance it?
MARYBETH Not real well, but I try!

Lesson 19 **Sounds, activity 1**

1. He's much smarter than I am.
2. She's as intelligent as he is.
3. Her clothes are different from mine.
4. She has the same shoes as I have.
5. Sandals are less common here than in Florida.
6. Kids are more casual than their parents.

Lesson 19 **Sounds, activity 2**

1. He's less casual than she is.
   No, he's *more* casual than she is.
2. It's noisier now than it was.
   No, it's *less* noisy now than it was.
3. Clothes are cheaper here than at home.
   No, clothes are *less* cheap here than at home.
4. He's less optimistic than she is.
   No, he's *more* optimistic than she is.
5. It's easier to get good clothes here.
   No, it's *less* easy to get good clothes here.
6. He's less confident than she is.
   No, he's *more* confident than she is.

Lesson 19 **Listening and Speaking, activity 2**

Q Where are you from originally, Don?

DON Well, I grew up in Valdez, Alaska. My folks still live there, but I moved to New York to study fashion design, and then came here to San Francisco six years ago.

Q Have you traveled much outside of the U.S.?

DON Oh sure! Europe, of course, and Japan, Korea, Thailand—lots of places in Asia. And Mexico, Jamaica, Cuba…

Q Well, how would you describe the way Americans dress?

DON Hmmm. Well, it depends on the season, of course, and the area, but I'd have to say "casual" in general. People dress much more casually in the West than in the East, I think, but jeans are still the most popular clothes, wherever you go—and people wear them for everything.

Q Even to work?

DON Well, I guess it depends on the business, but yes. I guess most people wear suits and ties—formal clothes—for work, and for church, or if they go out for a nice dinner…

Q Are nice clothes expensive?

DON Not really. Not compared to, say, Italy or Japan. But in terms of how much people earn, they're… umm… they're probably about the same, relatively.

Q OK. And what about casual clothes—are they expensive?

DON No, not at all. Did you know a pair of Levis 501s cost three times more in Tokyo than in San Francisco?

Q No kidding! Umm… What do you think of the quality of clothes design in the U.S.?

DON Oh, I think we have some fantastic designers here, not just in terms of fashion, but in terms of practicality and quality.

Q Tell me, would you say Americans are small or large people, compared to other people around the world?

DON Well, uh… there are some really tall people around, and you see a lot more overweight people here than in most other countries. Food is cheap… and good!

Lesson 20 **Listening, activity 1**

Q So, what was your most memorable journey, Sarah?

SARAH Well, in 1990 I drove across country with a friend who was moving home from New Orleans to Laguna Beach on the California coast.

Q Mmm. How long did it take?

SARAH Oh… nine days, I think.

Q What sort of distance is that?

SARAH About 2,500 miles, and that's pretty direct, too.

Q So where did you go?

SARAH Well, we set out from New Orleans and took the Interstate 10 Highway, which runs all the way from Florida to Los Angeles. We got on it just outside the city, and we drove through Louisiana as far as San Antonio in Texas, where we stopped for the night.

Q How far was that?

SARAH Oh, the first day we did 550 miles.

Q What's San Antonio like?

SARAH It's pretty interesting. It's a strange mix of skyscrapers and Indian houses and churches. It's about 200 years old.

Q What's the scenery like in the country? Is it desert or mountainous or what?

SARAH Well, it's not really mountainous at that point, it's um… sort of hills and small trees. It's very remote, though, and you can drive hundreds of miles between gas stations, so you have to make sure you've got plenty of gas.

Q It was cheaper then, wasn't it?

SARAH Yes, it cost about a dollar a gallon, about 40 cents less than now.

Q And, where did you go then?

SARAH Well, after that, we started to hit the desert and we drove 350 miles to Fort Stockton, which is a typical desert motel stop, in the middle of nowhere. Then we drove through the Guadeloupe Mountains National Park to El Paso, on the border between Texas and Mexico. Then between El Paso and Las Cruces you start climbing into the Sierra Madre.

Q And that was when you could only drive at 55 miles an hour?

SARAH Yeah. Of course we went a lot faster. If there were no police patrols around.

Q Where to then?

SARAH We turned off and took a detour to Nogales on the Mexican border which was great. We had lunch there, and then headed north to Tucson, Arizona on Route 19.

Q And where did you stay on the way?

SARAH In motels. They were really cheap. The most expensive was 35 dollars, the cheapest was twenty. And from Tucson we turned west again and crossed into California. From there it's only 300 miles to San Diego on the coast, which was very beautiful—my first sight of the Pacific Ocean. And then we drove on up the Pacific Coast Highway to Laguna Beach, not far from L.A., and arrived at my friend's apartment, with a fabulous sea view and only ten minutes from the beach.

Q It sounds very memorable!

SARAH It was, it really was. But although it was great to arrive, it was much better to travel. We had a blast!

Fluency 4 **Listening and Speaking, activity 2**

A It's my birthday today.

B Congratulations! Did you get any presents?

A Yes, I got a neat pair of socks.

B Socks! What a fantastic present! Anything else?

A Yes, I also got some nice handkerchiefs. They're just what I've always wanted.

B And are you going to do anything to celebrate?

A Yes, I'm going for a walk in the park.

B You sure are celebrating in style! Have a wonderful time.

A Thank you.

Fluency 4 **Listening, activity 1**

Q OK, Judy, can you tell us something about holidays in the United States?

JUDY Sure. Well, I think probably the most important holiday is Thanksgiving. That's always on the last Thursday of November. And it's a time when families get together to say thank you for, well, for all the good things they have enjoyed in the past year. Um, the original Thanksgiving meal was held by the first settlers in the United States. To say thank you to God for their first successful harvest and to say thank you to the Native Americans who helped them survive their first year here.

Q So, basically it's a meal?

JUDY Well, yes, it's the one time in the year when families get together and they cook a big meal, and yes, I think the meal is the most important part of the holiday. We have turkey and pumpkin pie and ...

Q Mmm sounds delicious. How about other holidays? For example when is Labor Day?

JUDY Oh, Labor Day is the first Monday in September. It doesn't commemorate anything in particular, but it's the official end of the summer.

Q And do you do anything special? Are there any special customs on Labor Day?

JUDY No, not really. It's a national holiday so we all have the day off. But there are no special customs or celebrations.

Q How about Valentine's Day?

JUDY Well, that's on February 14th. That's the day when you send a card to the person you love. And it's the day when you can reveal your love to someone who perhaps doesn't know that you love them.

Q And how do you do that?

JUDY Well, traditionally you don't sign the card so the person who gets it has to guess who it's from. And so they find out that there is someone out there who loves them. Sometimes there's a poem in the card. You know, roses are red, violets are blue, this card comes from the one who loves you!

Q Right! Do you give gifts on Valentine's Day?

JUDY Oh, yes, flowers and chocolates usually. And if you're in a relationship, you would probably go out for a romantic dinner.

Q And do Americans know who St. Valentine was?

JUDY I don't think so. I don't think they think about the origins of the day at all. This is just the day when we celebrate being in love. Oh, and it's not really a holiday—you don't get the day off—it's just another working day.

Q OK. Another big holiday is Independence Day, July 4th. Can you tell us something about that?

JUDY Yes, of course, Independence Day is a big holiday. It's when we celebrate our Independence from Britain, you know after the War of Independence in 1776, when the United States first became an independent country. It's in the summer on July 4th so we have picnics and ball games, fireworks, parades. It's really quite something.

Q Finally, what about Mother's Day. Is that big in the States?

JUDY Oh, yes, that's big over here. Particularly for the flower sellers.

Q So you give flowers to your mom?

JUDY Oh, yes, we give flowers and cards and sometimes a present. To say thank you to our mom for having raised us and looked after us all those years.

Q And when is Mother's Day?

JUDY Well, I think it's the second Sunday in May.

Q Well, thanks very much.

JUDY You're welcome.

Macmillan Education
Between Towns Road, Oxford OX4 3PP, UK
A division of Macmillan Publishers Limited
Companies and representatives throughout the world

ISBN 0 435 29756 2

Text © Simon Greenall 1997
First published 1997
Design and illustration © Macmillan Publishers Limited 1998

Heinemann is a registered trademark of Reed Educational & Professional Publishing Limited

Designed by Stafford and Stafford
Cover design by Stafford and Stafford

Illustrations by:

Adrian Barclay (Beehive Illustration), p. 30; Martin Sanders, pp. 14, 20, 21, 27, 32, 36, 40, 42/43, 56; Simon Smith, pp. 13, 29, 53; Stafford & Stafford, pp. 45, 47.

Commissioned photography by:
Chris Honeywell pp. 18, 44, 48/49.

Author's acknowledgements

I am very grateful to all the people who have contributed towards the creation of this book. My thanks are due to:

- All the teachers I have had the privilege to meet on seminars in many different countries and the various people who have influenced my work.
- Paul Ruben for producing the tapes, and the actors for their voices.
- The various schools who piloted the material.
- Simon Stafford for the stunning design of the book.
- James Hunter and Bridget Green for their careful attention to detail and their creative contribution.
- Clare Leeds for her careful management of the project.
- Helena Gomm for her patient and good-humored editorial input.
- And last, but by no means least, Jill, Jack, and Alex.

Acknowledgements

The authors and publishers would like to thank the following for their kind permission to reproduce copyright material in this book:

Doubleday, a division of Bantam Doubleday Dell Publishing Group Inc. for an extract from *American Express A Century of Service* by Alden Hatch. © 1950 by Harlan Logan; Desmond Morris for an extract from *The Book of Ages* published by Jonathan Cape Ltd.; Penguin Putnam Inc. for an adapted extract from *A Life on the Road* by Charles Kuralt. © 1990 by Charles Kuralt; Rogers, Coleridge and White Ltd. on behalf of Stephen Pile for an extract from *Cannibals in the Cafeteria*. © 1988 by Stephen Pile.

The authors and publishers would like to thank the following for permission to reproduce their material: Adams Picture Library p. 52; Allsport/Bill Hickey p. 29; AMEX p. 19; Jeanne Hebuterne by Modigliani, Amedeo (1884–1920) Christie's Images/Bridgeman Art Library, London p. 46 (t); Self portrait (Adelaide Road), 1939 by Spencer, Stanley (1891–1959) Ex-Edward James Foundation, Sussex/Bridgeman Art Library, London p. 47 (t); Britstock IFA pp. 8 (t), 38, 39; Colorific pp. 4 (b), 8 (b), 16/17; The Girl With a Red Hat by Jan Vermeer, Francis G. Mayer/Corbis p. 46 (b); Doisneau/Rapho/Network p. 10; Hulton Getty p. 16; Image Bank pp. 3 (t), 4 (t); Images Colour Library pp. 50/51, 54, 55; Impact Photos p. 50; Pictor International p. 25 (b); Superstock pp. 6, 22/23; Self-Portrait in Grey Felt Hat by Vincent Van Gogh, Superstock p. 46 (m); Tony Stone Images pp. 2, 3 (b), 34/35; Telegraph Colour Library p. 24/25.

The publishers would like to thank: American Express

Printed in Thailand

2006 2005 2004 2003 2002
16 15 14 13 12 11 10 9 8